THE SUBURBAN MANIFESTO

How To Make City Hall
Do Exactly What You Want

By

Joe B. Vaughan, Jr.

ISBN: 1452800065

EAN-13: 9781452800066

Cover graphics by Pete Hall (pete.hall@sbcglobal.net)

Acknowledgements

Many thanks to everyone who helped make this project possible, most especially:

My brave readers Mike McEachern, John Zacharias, Brandy Adams, Charles "Boomer" Rice, Doug Havemann, Ariel Wakeland, Frank Whetstine (www.sikpik.com), Cassie Byard, Rick Davis, Jody Sheppard, Jason Cain, Bob Adams (no relation to Brandy), Jeff Lockhart, Christy Goldfinch, and last but not least, my mom Alethea Vaughan.

My superlative agent, Carol Givner (www.goldduets.com).

My amazing baristas at the Midlothian Starbucks who bring the magic elixir that makes my fingers dance across the laptop keys.

Thank you!

In memory of my good friend, Doug Steeb.

For Suse

Introduction

What is the most invasive form of government in the United States? Which one can most directly, most effectively, mess with your life, your family, your house, your pets, your likes, your dislikes, your habits, your tolerance of other people's habits, almost everything about you, every day, every moment, 24/7?

The American federal government? That massive, enormous, indifferent bureaucracy managing labyrinthine social programs, a huge military and formidable, covert, intimidating security agencies monitoring your phone calls, email, and texts via secret, exotic technologies - all for your protection?

1

Got to be the feds, right?

Wrong.

The only thing the American federal government spends more energy and wealth on than cultivating its appearance as powerful, mighty, omnipresent and infallible is maintaining a safe distance from constituents. Distance maximizes the federal mystique. Distance also reduces interaction with most Americans to a single, mandatory instance.

April 15th.

If you are a registered voter, you might actually increase your interaction with your federal government two- or three-fold during election years, if you choose to participate in the primaries and general elections to select congresspersons, senators, and sometimes presidents.

But increasing dissatisfaction with elected representation in Washington has effectively beaten back political fervor in most Americans. Many voters feel so disenfranchised with their federal government, with the actions of their elected officials that the percentage of Americans still participating in our republic is minuscule compared to the overall number of registered voters. The ranks of unregistered voters are even larger – good people who see the political process in this country as too distant, unresponsive and pointless to matter.

This disengagement, some would say at the pleasure and advantage of Washington, leaves the single, mandatory annual tax deadline as the only direct interaction many, maybe most Americans still have with their federal government.

Even if you rely on some form of federal entitlement or aid, work for, do business with, or run a business heavily regulated by the government, direct federal intervention in your life is still mostly a business hours-only proposition.

In fact, the largest group of Americans enduring anything close to fulltime federal interaction is the proud, honorable women and men protecting our country in the US armed forces. But, for the most part, even that consists only of their on-duty time.

Nope. Ultimately, with a few exceptions, the only people in America who could boast a truly intimate 24/7-relationship with our national government are the inhabitants of the loftiest positions in the Congressional, Judicial, or Executive branches, and anyone incarcerated in a federal facility.

Interesting.

So, what is the most intrusive form of government in the US? Which one can and does touch your life directly almost every single moment of every single day? Who governs the purity of the water you drink? Who allows the cable company to operate as a monopoly and dictate your television experience?

Who determines whether you may smoke in public or not, and if so, where you may smoke? Who provides or denies you mass transit service? Who decides the appropriate number and types of animals you may keep as pets? Who decides what animals you may not keep as pets?

Who decides how many libraries you may have? Who decides what books your libraries may lend? Who decides if your libraries may have computers and who decides what Internet sites one may surf on those computers?

Who decides if you may buy alcohol, what type of alcohol, where you may buy it if you may?

Who determines the appropriate number of police and fire personnel to adequately protect you and your family while you sleep? Who decrees what equipment the fire department may use? Who mandates what type of weapons, what caliber bullets, the police department may deploy, and how they may deploy them?

Who operates the digital cameras monitoring your driving habits through almost every intersection? Who decides who gets to see the digital photography captured by those cameras, and what is ultimately done with those pictures? Who?

City hall.

Formidable. Mysterious. Astonishingly powerful. Your local municipal government. The list of all activities for which your city hall is responsible is staggering. It could go on and on and on without naming all the ways your city can touch your life, every single moment, every single day.

"You can't fight City Hall!" the old saying goes, probably created by the same political mindset that brought us "You shouldn't swap horses in mid stream."

I don't know much about horses in streams, but I think the point of that slogan is to advocate keeping current political leaders in place, no matter what, because the alternative, the terrifying "unknown", might be even worse.

Bullshit.

Second only to the idea that we have the right to elect people to public office to represent our wishes is the idea that we have the right to replace anyone who *does not* represent our wishes, especially anyone who promises to act on our collective behalf then fails miserably to do so. Boot those bastards first! Make them examples for anyone even remotely considering employment as a professional politician.

It's your right.

City hall belongs to you. It is inhabited, some would say infested, with local politicians and other questionable associates, but *city hall belongs to you.*

It does not belong to the politicians who, after a little time in office begin to feel they are ordained to make decisions, spend tax money, and pontificate without regard to you, your family, your neighbors or anyone. Well, anyone except the other people who seem to constantly occupy city hall; the people who make their livings - some of them make exorbitant livings, by the way - lobbying your local government.

City hall lobbyists? Yup. Down there every day, buttonholing your elected representatives, pushing big plans and making big money while the rest of us are busy earning our livings and paying taxes to support a lobbyist-friendly environment in city hall.

"Not in my town!" you say? Look and see and if you find politicians blinded by the glitz of easy money flowing from developers and big businesses and power companies and anyone needing city council approval to turn a mondo profit, it's your duty to kick your representatives to the curb and get new ones. New reps that will put your interests first.

That's what I did in the early-1990s. I led a very successful political revolt in Irving, Texas - a full scale, legal, highly satisfying, democratic coup against an ineffective, corrupt municipal government.

My co-conspirators and I – that is *exactly* the way the sitting Irving city council and their cronies viewed us – selected, endorsed, supported and helped elect an entire slate of candidates; five of seven council seats, to vote our will as a majority bloc to stop city hall from providing a safe haven for developers drooling over massive, exorbitant, lead pipe chinch-profits derived through their cozy relationships with Irving's political establishment.

During a fiery speech I gave before the council prior to the municipal election, I referred to these huge profits from overdevelopment in Irving as *obscene*. They *were* obscene because these developers felt they were owed their profits regardless of the impact to anyone victimized by their projects.

My use of the word so incensed one developer in the audience he rose to his feet and charged me while I spoke at the city council guest podium - he required physical restraint from his lawyers and subordinates.

Undaunted, I continued my speech, labeling the nearly 1000% profit from a proposed zoning change that would clog streets near my home with traffic and extend wait time into double digits for emergency services as absolutely obscene. I completed my invective by turning and asking this developer if he knew a better definition for the word. If so, I wanted to hear it.

I am still waiting.

He had lots of developer and lobbyist friends. Hundreds it seemed, all growing wealthy ruining my city, making millions of dollars then running back their fine houses in their exclusive neighborhoods, far from ghastly projects like the ones they wanted to force on my neighborhood; impervious because wherever these bastards lived, they enjoyed good zoning, protecting their homes and families from developers just like them.

Bad developers grown fat, secure and rich from profits on horrid ventures my city hall habitually blessed without a second thought.

My city hall. My local governmental officials supposedly "sworn" to put the interests of me, my friends, my neighbors, everyone living in our city, ahead of anyone else – especially anyone who might come to town and threaten our happiness, our safety, our lives.

The same politicians I made sure were replaced in the next election.

I used numerous appearances at the podium before city council questioning the logic and motivation behind approving what seemed to me, a reasonably educated person, so many terrible ideas.

I questioned openly, at high volume. I wanted the question asked. I wanted there to be a public record of the discussion. I wanted the mayor and council to know someone was watching. I wanted my local elected officials to feel the political targets my fellow revolutionaries and I were drawing on their backs.

My co-conspirators and I worked for nearly a year to challenge our city council to do better. When they refused, we replaced five of the seven councilpersons who continually voted lockstep to make these developer fat cats richer, happier, more comfortable in their pursuit of the American dream, all under the guise of "highest and best use" - the supposition in real estate that the best use of any property is whatever produces the highest profit, regardless, as we became aware, of the impact to anyone or anything else in the vicinity.

My comrades and I used our issue, the uncontrolled overdevelopment of our city, to galvanize public support to stop the corrupt municipal death spiral we saw going on around us.

And for a reasonable time – all politicians have a limited shelf life; hence the need for across-the-board term limitations for *every* politician, no matter the position - our new city council did exactly what we wanted them to do. We ruled.

You can too.

This is a cookbook; useful instructions on how you can take control of your local government. A design manual for employing your rights effectively to get what you want, taking no prisoners in the process.

A working plan to properly utilize that frightening, empowering moment when you realize that whether you participate or not, your local government is going to approve and enforce laws that will directly affect your life, while conducting business and spending your tax money in ways you may oppose ethically and morally.

The only way to stop them is to participate in the system, take it over if necessary then make some changes.

My personal struggle with city hall described in this book focuses on zoning issues; one of the biggest problems most people face with their local governments.

But even if your issue isn't zoning related, the organization and presentation techniques I describe here are useful for effectively taking your fight down to your city government and getting what you want.

It's your right, and if you organize similarly to the way I did, you can exercise your rights so effectively that city hall will have no choice but to do exactly as you demand. That's their job. You just have to remind them who's the boss. That's your job.

Fighting for change takes time. It takes effort and thought. It can be a hassle. But it is *never* nearly as difficult as your local politicians and city officials will try to convince you it is. Consider that if local politics really was so difficult, why are your local politicians so successful at it?

The unfortunate truth is that most public servants, local or otherwise, are not great, gifted, intelligent leaders at all. They are just better versed in, more comfortable with, how your government works than you are. More experienced in manipulating bureaucratic protocol.

But, in the world of full-contact politics, an impassioned, agile, focused amateur can easily beat down a calloused, conformance-driven, unimaginative, ass-kissing politician. The secret is knowing how to properly, righteously, gleefully administer that beat down.

You are, after all, a good, sincere, incensed person working for a noble cause and armed with one of the most effective, most fearsome weapons ever devised by the human mind: *Democracy*. At city hall, there is no defense against democracy.

None.

Democracy wins. Simple math - you bring the most votes, you make the rules. The people who haunt your city hall – lobbyists, developers, touchy-feely power company reps and elected officials - all fear democracy. That's because democracy means change. It means the status quo, "business as usual", is being thrown over, and someone else is in control.

You.

Revolution is a challenge. Like anything good, it takes time and effort and dedication and the ability to sift through the smoke and mirrors and bullshit and stay true to yourself and your cause. What you want.

Believe it or not, politically you *deserve* what you want. You certainly deserve what you want much more than anyone looking to use your government to make a buck, especially if they don't care what happens to you or your rights in the process.

It feels good to kick these rude, indifferent bastards back into the shadows. It's a blast, in fact. Even more important, and I say this a lot, it is your right.

I'll tell how you to do it.

Joe B. Vaughan, Jr.

.

Nature of the Beast

Richard Nixon used the phrase "the silent majority" to infer that anyone not actively protesting against his administration *supported him and his policies.*

Using that logic, any Americans sitting quietly, whether they liked him or not, were by default loving Tricky Dickey and everything he stood for, everything he did, every single moment.

Politicians still believe this. In any government, silence is always creatively interpreted as approval.

The thing politicians don't tell you is that they intentionally make it as difficult as possible for constituents to communicate with them. Through history, politicians have utilized the thick protective shell of bureaucracy, specifically, *bureaucratic protocol*, adapted, evolved, augmented, enhanced, fattened, reinforced and raised to the level of a holy language.

A holy government language intended to intimidate anyone wishing to approach their elected officials to demand responsibility and change.

A holy government language/tap dance politicians hope is abstruse enough, intimidating enough, mind-numbing enough, to scare away all casual participation, leaving the synodical halls - the places where decisions are made, money is spent, obscene profits are ordained - quiet and businesslike.

Silence equals approval.

Equally important: Noise - in this case, unorganized political expression - is interpreted as ignorance. Immediately dismissible ignorance.

Consider this: You and I may be majorly pissed-off. We could be tightly united in being majorly pissed-off about everything going on in our government. About being ignored, subterfuged, sold short, lied to, or just plain used by our elected officials, especially when they endorse some action or program with which we do not, would never, ever agree.

And while we are entitled to use our first amendment rights to vent our political frustrations – screaming your disapproval in public does feel *really* good, by the way – choosing that mode of expression over a more effective, measured, articulate, apparently civil, bureaucratic protocol-defeating approach allows the people in power to label you as shrill, misguided, ignorant, possibly dangerous, orchestrated, and/or bused-in, while dismissing you and your message completely.

The privilege of power.

But, to beat protocol and get what you want politically, you must tell your story in an approachable, logical, effective way.

Message is almost everything. Almost. Message is second only to its necessary-evil cousin, *presentation.*

A very sad statement, but in our predigested-to-consumer-approachable-informational-chunk media landscape, absolutely true. A truth you must understand and master in your successful coup at city hall. We'll get to that in a minute.

First, some background.

Most city councils tend to evolve through four general phases over the history of a city:

Founding Fathers Phase – after a new town is incorporated, the initial city council, elected at-large, usually consists of the local prime movers, such as big land owners, bankers, etc.

Real Estate Agent Phase – after a town begins to grow, the founding fathers tend to surrender their council seats to local real estate agents, again elected at-large, and vitally, vehemently interested in controlling zoning of land inside the city limits, as well as annexation of property outside city limits.

There may also be a few doctors and lawyers and other people sprinkled into the mix here and there, but usually not too many. Real estate agents profit from the sale of property they represent, begging the question of conflict of interest when they sit on city council approving zoning.

Most real estate agents serving on city councils will say that they recuse themselves for any decisions profitable to them personally. But, obviously, their participation on city council cannot preclude the possibility for abuse.

Unfortunately, for most American cities, city councils dominated by real estate agents are often the norm, certainly shifting the focus of city planning and operation towards land acquisition and development, and away from other important concerns such as ensuring city priorities and services are focused equitably across all city residents.

Not to slight people in the real estate industry; for the most part, they are fine folks performing useful services for the rest of us. But their concentrations on city councils, along with the length the *Real Estate Phase* lasts in most city histories - usually far longer than the other phases - does pose some important questions about why municipal governments tend to fail so often in properly representing their constituents.

Chamber of Commerce Phase – after most of the land inside a city is zoned and developed, and any available adjacent land to the city is annexed and zoned/developed, the real estate agents tend to surrender their tenure on city council to local business leaders, usually still elected at-large and intent on using their time in office to promote business inside the city, attract new business and industry to the city, etc.

Single Member Districting Phase – this phase can occur at any time in the lifespan of a city's government, the sooner the better, and requires residents to approve a referendum to divide the city into districts. Afterwards voters inside each district elect their own councilperson.

This phase is the usual mode of operation in most large American cities, where residents require more familiarity with, and accountability from their councilpersons than is possible with at-large representation.

The city council evolutionary pattern listed above is offered only as a general guide to help you determine the motivations behind the decisions your local elected officials may be making on your behalf, and how best to plan your revolt to effectively change your city government.

Most municipal governments come in two flavors: *Mayor-Council* or *Council-Manager*.

In the Mayor-Council configuration, the mayor controls city hall directly. This is often referred to as the strong-mayor council, a common arrangement for large cities such as New York City, where the mayor appoints department heads and managers who carry out her or his policy. The mayor runs the city.

There is a variation on Mayor-Council, known as the weak-mayor council, where the mayor holds the same power as any of the other councilpersons, while serving a ceremonial function, welcoming dignitaries, judging parades, cutting ribbons to open malls, etc. The entire council controls all city departments directly, appointing department managers to run the city.

In the Council-Manager configuration, the most common version of municipal government in America, a city manager, a professional municipal administrator, is hired by the city council to manage the city staff running the city on behalf of the mayor and council.

In Council-Manager cities, the mayor and council vote to approve their public policies then instruct the city manager to implement their decisions.

Why is this important?

To effectively assault your city hall, you need to know who's really running the show. Is it the mayor and a bunch of questionable associates? Is it a city council infested with political tools rubberstamping dreadful local laws to line the pockets of their developer friends? Is it someone else, perhaps not an elected official at all, sitting back, pulling the strings, watching the money rolling in?

Important questions.

Case in point: How I lost my first job as a journalist on a small daily newspaper in Texas. Any time I was ever employed as a newspaper journalist, I covered city hall. A city hall reporter.

Good for writing books like this. Also good because most journalists would rather be sports reporters or columnists than city hall reporters. Hence usually gainful employment, wading deep into all the good ol' boy network bullshit down at city hall. Loads of good ol' boy bullshit down there, believe me.

But I digress.

My first taste of professional municipal politics exposed me to one of the most corrupt people I've ever encountered.

In another side life, I have also been a working Texas bar musician, so, to infer that this man was the most corrupt person I've ever encountered is really saying something.

This man shall remain nameless, but he was the city manager in the town I was covering. By our first meeting, he'd already been city manager there for nearly 20 years. That is important because most city managers stay for 6 years or so before moving on to a bigger city and a higher salary.

Not this guy. He was making plenty of money right where he was, a by-product of the lucrative local and federal connections he'd developed during his 20 years as steward of "the interests of the people" - ergo, his stay well beyond his welcome.

This city manager was notorious for two things. First, on the wall over a sofa across his office from his desk hung a huge oil painting that, on first glance, looked like a large crowd on bleachers watching a football game.

The first time I interviewed him in his office, he explained that he was proud of his painting and that he allowed only a few people to inspect it closely.

He invited me to have a look, and after more scrutiny I noticed square in the middle of the painting, surrounded by hundreds of cheering people, a naked woman, her breasts clearly visible in the crowd.

"Now don't you go givin' away my secrets, huh?" he chuckled.

While I later sat in the guest chair in front of his desk pondering this strange canvas, he picked up his telephone and called a connection in Washington and asked for a cool $1 million in federal money to develop a "much needed" park in the south end of town.

What I was way too green to piece together there on my second day as a big time city hall reporter was that historically, the land he secured for federal park development grant money was usually in the local flood plain.

That meant that when the weather was good, the baseball diamonds, playgrounds and soccer fields were dry and useable. But if there were ever more than 2 or 3 hours of sustained rainfall, the city parks flooded.

In other words, the land he was buying for the park improvement projects he championed at election time when endorsing council candidates who would subsequently vote to renew his employment contract, was worthless. No one could build on the floodplain because the city couldn't zone development there.

He usually bought flood plain land for the city from one of his local friends; land for which his buddies had paid next to nothing. Then this city manager would fund construction of swing sets, a baseball diamond or two, send the mayor out to cut the blue ribbon, call another of his local chums - my boss, the newspaper publisher - to ensure front page coverage, and everybody was happy. Certainly not nearly $1 million happy, but hey, we had some new parks!

But hey, what happened to the rest of the money?

Yeah. I lost my first job as a journalist asking questions like that. Some people at city hall can get a little touchy, sometimes. And they do not play.

Fortunately for me, I managed to ask my professionally-fatal question after covering the election where local voters sent a whole slew of new councilpersons to city hall to fire this city manager.

The good townspeople, over the course of the city council campaign, had become keenly curious about the often-flooded municipal parkland, along with the startling revelation made by the local police association that there were only eight functioning police cars covering the city's nine police districts – a fact this city manager asked me not to report before the election because he said he feared robbers and criminals would read that news and plan accordingly.

The voters decided enough was enough. They wanted change, and they made it happen.

You can too.

The Irritation Threshold

The irritation threshold is the point where a person decides that an issue is so threatening, so terrible, so corrupt, ignorant, completely wrong, that she or he feels compelled to rise from the comfort of home and family and television and charge down to the government and throttle some stupid bastard - for the public good, of course.

When someone is irritated at or above this threshold - believes the threat is real to her or his family, home, neighborhood, city, country - that person becomes vehemently involved in the political process, seething, glaring, snarling, demanding change. The problem with this phenomenon is that the moment a person's irritation threshold subsides she or he usually disengages from the political process, wishing instead to spend time on much more pleasant pursuits such as life, family, home and friends.

Nothing wrong with that at all. Exactly how we all should spend our time. The problem is that the less attention we pay to our government, our elected representatives, the more they fail to represent us.

If everyone were just a little more aware, a little more involved, a little more cognoscente of what was happening around us politically, we could keep the politicians a little more honest, a little more responsive, and alleviate the irritation threshold as the flashpoint by which most Americans begin and end their political participation.

My irritation threshold manifested like this: I was enjoying a wonderful Sunday morning with a hot cup of coffee and the newspaper in my little house in Valley Ranch, a mixed-use neighborhood in northern Irving, Texas.

By mixed use I mean there were little single family houses like mine, larger single family houses up the street, multi-family apartments, office buildings, and other businesses, all co-existing more-or-less happily across the large, hill-encircled bowl known as Valley Ranch.

For example, the Dallas Cowboys offices and practice facilities were down the street from my house. Neighbors often commented on seeing different players jogging through the neighborhood after practice.

Near the Cowboys was the first Dallas Stars hockey practice rink. Never saw them jogging – more difficult in skates I suppose, but you get the picture.

This made for an interesting mix of activities in this beautiful, appealing neighborhood - kept beautiful and appealing by mandatory monthly dues my neighbors and I paid to the homeowners association for landscaping and maintenance.

Our dues also supported similar maintenance for the numerous commercial properties surrounding us, something few of us realized prior to our revolution.

Association-subsidized curb appeal combined with Irving's central location in the vast Dallas/Ft. Worth Metroplex made my neighborhood highly desirable among area commuters.

The downside to living in my neighborhood was rush hour. Twice every weekday, nearly-gridlocked rush hour traffic clogged McArthur Boulevard, the only road in or out of Valley Ranch; six-lanes running north-south through the entire neighborhood.

Even with a local fire station located near the middle of Valley Ranch, my neighbors and I were pretty much out-of-luck if stricken by heart attack, fire, or any other need for emergency services during morning or evening rush hour.

During those periods, emergency responders had no choice but to join the creeping traffic because along many sections of the busy main boulevard, there was nowhere for the other vehicles to go to make way for ambulances and fire trucks. An incredibly dangerous situation.

The price of success, the neighborhood association said. With the popularity of our neighborhood bringing in so many new residents, we'd all just have to bear the inconvenience until more access was developed down through the surrounding hills. But with a lake on the west side of Valley Ranch and the Trinity River winding around the east, MacArthur Boulevard was, and remains to this day, the only way in or out.

But on that Sunday morning, my coffee was fresh and hot and I wasn't driving anywhere and life was good. Right up until the moment my eyes crossed an article in the *Dallas Morning News* about the record number of multi-family zoning requests currently en route to the Irving City Council, a majority of this development planned for the remaining hills and open spaces in my neighborhood, Valley Ranch.

The article included the astonishing revelation that Irving held the dubious distinction of being among American cities with the highest apartment densities in the United States.

My mind reeled. I immediately imagined all of the apartments in New York City and Chicago and San Francisco and other huge cities across the country. And here was Irving right up there with them, with the council seriously considering allowing hundreds, if not thousands more.

No wonder traffic sucked.

Now, don't get me wrong. I have nothing against apartments and absolutely nothing against the good people living in apartments. I've lived in several apartments. I lived in an apartment in Irving before buying my little house there. Apartments and apartment residents are fine with me and absolutely not the trigger for my irritation threshold.

Not a bit.

The point of my alarm, along with all the people with whom I subsequently came into contact in this political adventure - *many of them apartment residents* - was the very real, very dangerous problem created by a shocking lack of planning on behalf of our local government.

A problem of which my local elected officials seemed unaware, or refused to acknowledge. McArthur Boulevard could no longer support the traffic from the existing development there. Now the city was poised to approve even high densities, apparently with no regard for the impact it would have on my neighbors, my friends or me.

This municipal mindset indicated even larger problems. I knew from my previous life as a city hall reporter that in order to guarantee adequate city service, i.e., police protection, fire protection, ambulance, water, sewer, etc, most cities strictly enforce a ratio of roughly 10% multi-family to 90% single-family development.

Higher multi-family ratios make planning and budgeting for city services nearly impossible because the population the city government must support over, for example, a 10-year period, cannot be accurately estimated; too many people moving in and out of town on a continual basis. This shifting population also impacts local schools trying to properly educate and support a constantly changing number of students.

Surely my city was already at or near the upper density limit for this type of development. How could the council possibly be considering approving more?

Equally problematic is the nearly perpetual resale of multi-family properties: It is very common for apartment complexes to be flipped every two to three years.

It is also very common for subsequent owners to invest less than their predecessors to maintain these properties, *especially in markets where new apartments spring up continually*, forcing older complexes to reduce rental fees to remain competitive, lowering revenue and property taxes for the city - less money for fire and police protection, along with other essential city services, now stretched over a larger, more dense city population.

What the hell was going on? If the council was aware of the problems we residents were already having, why were they even considering sacrificing the safety of my neighbors and me for the sake of such obvious overdevelopment?

Was anyone in control?

I pounded my breakfast table, spilled some of my delicious coffee, paced around and tried to organize my previous journalistic experience into some kind of logical response.

My mind returned to the same conclusion: There was so much location-based demand for my city and my neighborhood that the council couldn't stop this development.

Or, they didn't want to.

Fire raced through my head – my irritation threshold.

I stomped around some more, raving, swearing to go right down there and tell those city hall bastards exactly what I thought about them. They'd listen to me, goddamnit!

I scanned the newspaper article until I saw that the next city council meeting was a week from Tuesday.

Perfect. Week from Tuesday. I poured more coffee and pondered a new thought, fresh in from the flames of my ire. I pay my mandatory homeowner's association dues. Shouldn't the association have a lawyer or someone to go down and pound city hall for me?

That led to me to wonder what my association might have done previously on my behalf - obviously not very much if things had already degenerated to the current state.

Damn!

I called someone I knew connected with the association. She told me that while the organization was aware of the pending zoning change requests, due to potential exposure to litigation, my association could not send a formal representative to the meeting on behalf of the residents paying mandatory dues each month.

I expressed my dismay.

My friend told me I was the fifth or sixth person she'd heard from about the newspaper article in the previous 10 minutes. I told her I refused to let the issue go, first requesting she officially note my anger to our homeowner's association.

Then I told her I would be happy to host a meeting in my home the following Tuesday, a week before the council meeting, for anyone wanting to address this issue with the Irving City Council. She said she'd be there, and would pass the word.

My revolution began.

Joe B. Vaughan, Jr.

You Only Get One Shot

Message is almost everything. Almost. Message is second only to its necessary-evil cousin, *presentation*.

Despite numerous reports of my laziness, I repeat that here for emphasis. As we discussed previously, politicians creatively interpret unorganized political expression, especially heartfelt, genuine railing as noise.

To be effective in laying the groundwork for your revolution, you must first decide how best to organize your message so that even elected political officials can understand exactly what you are saying.

It's all in the approach. The appearance. The horrible showbiz aspect of everything in our culture. But if you want to get what you want, you have to work the system more effectively than the people in power. Fortunately, they're not very smart. You are, and you're motivated. Organize and focus!

The day after reading about the out-of-control zoning in Irving, I noticed an interesting, anonymous, copied-multiple-times sheet of paper stuck in my mailbox.

Someone else in my neighborhood was angry about the proposed zoning changes. Big pissed-enough to rant for line after line citing all the traffic problems, the increased response times for fire and police and ambulance service, all the negative impact the proposed zoning changes would bring to our lives. On and on and on - all wonderful, articulate points.

My friend on the homeowner's association called soon after, quoting the page she'd found in her mailbox, wondering if I'd had anything to do with it.

I couldn't take any credit, but I was very happy other neighbors were thinking along the same lines as me. Thinking *and* acting. Someone copied the hell out of this flyer, stuck it in hundreds of mailboxes, and it was generating some buzz.

Perfect.

I reaffirmed my plan to hold a meeting at my house to organize for the upcoming council meeting. I reminded my association-connected friend to tell everyone she knew that at 7PM the following night, I wanted a house full of alarmed, incensed, generally pissed-off people ready to march on city hall.

She told me no problem. She was already using her telephone tree to spread the word.

Telephone tree. God, what a weapon!

All through your revolution, but especially at the beginning, communication is the most important organizational tool you have. You must establish, nurture, feed, develop and grow your communication network. And to be effective, it cannot be your job alone.

There is no way for you, with your busy life, earning a living, supporting your home and family, being who you are, to get the message out to everyone who needs to know that you are working to change a political problem, and what they should be doing to help you.

You have to delegate, and you have to pick dependable people – people you know will do what they have to do – to get your message out. These are your co-conspirators. Your comrades. Your peeps. Your troops.

Got to have them, and you've got to trust that they will do what you ask them to do. Your revolution lives or dies based upon the number of people you enlist to work for your cause, carry your message, vote for the change you demand.

Fortunately, today we have major technological conveniences, most especially the Internet, to get everyone in your movement on the same page.

Using the free social networking sites available, you can post information faster and more accurately than the local media. You can tweet meeting plans and details so that everyone in your movement knows what to do, where to be. Essential communication.

But you are still faced with one preliminary daunting task. You must first make everyone else infuriated by your issue, the irritation threshold for your movement, aware of how to get the information they need to participate effectively. Where you are meeting, why you are meeting, etc.

That's where techniques like the telephone tree come in. Fortunately for me, my homeowner's association friend had a master telephone list of everyone else in the association.

She'd also already heard from several angry people and when I volunteered my house for our first meeting, she made ten calls to friends, all possessing her same telephone list.

She delegated 30 names to each of her ten friends, with instructions to briefly describe the issue then the location and time for the meeting. Very effective.

If you don't have a master telephone list, begin your movement by going door-to-door in your neighborhood. Talk to your neighbors face-to-face. Make them aware of your issue, the reason you have been moved to take action.

You'll be amazed how many of them have similar concerns, how many have been waiting for someone like you to come along and kick an effective response into motion.

From this beginning, this initial discussion among your friends and neighbors, send your message out to resonate through your neighborhood by getting your people to talk to their friends. Get them to discuss your issue with other people they know. Make your message grassroots and viral. Make it easy and logical to join your revolution.

Again, if your issue is important enough to motivate you, you'll find many others ready to organize and focus on the needed changes.

If each neighbor, each person you speak to, contacts just two people, and those two contact two more, etc. your movement will begin to grow so quickly that gathering a master telephone list will be the least of your concerns.

Motivated people need objectives. Gather them, identify your goals then get to work.

Oh yeah - get their telephone numbers too!

Within two hours of invoking the telephone tree, my phone was ringing off the wall. Upset people ranting and yelling, all ready to go downtown and take on the council.

Revolutionaries.

Timing Is . . . Well, You Know

To maximize your effectiveness as an *activist* - that's what you are now, a true champion for your cause before your local government - you must first develop your awareness of what issues your city council is considering.

In fact, you must stay well ahead of the city council at every opportunity, because, while official city policy isn't made until the council votes, the issues behind that policy are usually first considered, and recommendations made, pro or con, at the committee/board/commission level long before the council ever sees them.

Even in small cities, keeping up with all the decisions under consideration at city hall is daunting. Fortunately, thanks to the Internet, most cities list their committees, meeting schedules, and meeting agendas on their municipal web sites.

You can also grab committee listings and agendas at city hall, usually provided by the city secretary's office. If you don't see what you need, ask the city staff – that's what they are there for. From my experience, city staffers are friendly, and genuinely interested in anyone interested in the workings of city government, so ask away. They will help you if they can.

Another must-have source for city issues is a regular, comprehensive scan of your local newspaper. Again, the Internet is essential.

Most newspapers offer online, *searchable* versions of their hard copy editions. Search city hall and local politics, for example, or library, parks, police funding, etc. based on your area of interest.

A useful benefit of the online editions is that they often list links to local political reporters' blogs. This is a great way to stay informed on upcoming issues, as well as which writer(s) is covering which area in city hall. Good to know.

But you have to make the effort. If you want to change your city, change the percentage of city funding to support better parks or libraries, for example, or maybe to support more efficient use of city resources for better care and housing of the homeless, you must find the committees advising and making recommendations to city council on these issues then go there to make your interest and opinion known.

You have far more influence urging your positive changes through proactive participation than reactive panic.

As I will discuss later, reactive panic and righteous indignation are effective too. They have their place in the local political process, but they almost always encounter stiff resistance, followed by quick dismissal if not presented in an effective, coordinated manner, and with lots of muscle.

If you have the opportunity, stay ahead of your issue. If a city board or committee is meeting to discuss something important to you, attend that meeting. Participate in the discussion. Meet the board/committee members. Ask them to keep you posted on what they are considering. That's their job.

It's also your right.

Get to know your local media too. Call your city hall reporter(s). Introduce yourself at the next council meeting. Ask her or him what important issues need your scrutiny.

Some reporters may seem standoffish at first, but deep down they love talking to people who read and appreciate their work. They are also, for the most part, huge caffeine enthusiasts, so offer to buy them a cup to broaden your knowledge of the local political environment.

After cagy writers realize you are seeking to improve your understanding, not attempting to influence their objectivity, they will usually help you educate yourself.

This is also a very good way to forge necessary relationships with the media you will need when you take your revolution to the streets. Good press is essential. More on this later.

In my revolution, I fought against zoning allowing rampant overdevelopment that threatened to ruin my home and my neighborhood. Again, while the tactics and techniques described in this book refer in large part to my zoning-related combat, *they are completely applicable to any change you may wish to bring about in your local government.*

Zoning change requests are submitted by developers, property owners, etc. to the Planning and Zoning Commission (P&Z) long before the council ever receives the request for a formal vote.

Zoning change requests are necessary when a land plat within city jurisdiction is zoned for a particular use or category of uses, and the landowner or developer wants to change or adjust that zoning to allow a different use.

For example, a developer wants to build an office complex on a plat zoned for light industrial usage. If the city's light industrial zoning definition excludes office complexes, the developer must request a zoning change to allow the development project.

As part of the zoning change request process, P&Z must notify anyone on adjacent property who may be affected. Most cities specify mandatory notification within a certain radius of the proposed change, say 300 feet.

When a zoning change is requested the city usually posts a sign on the property announcing the change request then mails notices to everyone within the notification radius describing the requested change, and inviting anyone interested/impacted to attend the P&Z meeting at the time and place listed on the notice.

If you receive such a notice and have a concern, it is *vital* you attend the P&Z meeting for two important reasons:

First, as mentioned previously, the function of P&Z is to advise city hall on which zoning changes the council should approve, and which they should deny.

If you and your neighbors and fellow co-conspirators show up at the P&Z meeting and convince the P&Z commissioners that you believe the proposed zoning change will negatively impact you, your family and your property value, you have the opportunity to influence P&Z to advise the city council to deny the zoning change.

City council doesn't have to follow the recommendations of P&Z, but a recommendation for denial is good ammunition when you are building a case before council to kill a bad zoning request.

Second, when a zoning case goes before city council for a vote, and you voice your opposition, a common response by any smart-assed councilperson seeking to dismiss your argument is "Where were you when this change was requested at P&Z?"

The implication is that you have no right to waste the council's time if you didn't care enough to raise your concerns at the committee/board/commission level.

This assertion is pompous, wrong and meant to intimidate you. Don't be intimidated. You have every right to state your case. But, be mindful that some councilpersons love to bully constituents - again, the very people these politicians represent. Take names and vote accordingly. That's what I did.

I certainly would have spoken up much sooner, expressed my alarm and outrage before my P&Z commissioners, possibly swayed their recommendation, had I been more aware of the city plans for overdeveloping my neighborhood.

Instead I had to act from a position of surprise, from a position of defense, play catch up, and with very little time after reading the zoning article in my Sunday paper.

You can give yourself and your fellow revolutionaries the luxury of time and cool logic. All you have to do is open your eyes and act *before* your issue becomes critical. The earlier you are aware of issues under consideration at city hall, the more influence you have in the decision-making process.

Most people are floored by the poor attendance of most committee/board/commission meetings, along with how willing the panel members are to listen to *anyone* who chooses to participate.

The idea of a resident being interested and concerned enough to attend a committee meeting is a powerful thing to panel members, especially because they usually see little, if any, public interest in the issues they consider.

Use this to your advantage, especially for controversial decisions where an impassioned presentation from a group of concerned residents can help justify a recommendation the panel might have otherwise been hesitant to make.

Stay aware. Timing is everything.

Conspiracy

I was asleep. Unaware. The news that provoked me to act snuck up on me, stealthy, devious, waiting in that timely article in that Sunday newspaper to see if anyone was paying attention. Waiting to see who could imagine how our happy little world and happy little neighborhood and happy little homes would change if the status quo continued.

Business as usual.

I was lazy. I didn't expect or want any of the political adventure about to sweep into my life. I ignored the opportunity to stay ahead of the issue. That left me with only my initial frenzied reaction;

that angry fire, hot and hard to focus, racing through my head as I read the *Metro* section of *The Dallas Morning News* that Sunday morning.

Fortunately for me and my revolution, I also had my experience as a city hall reporter to temper my reaction. I knew city hall could have *very* little empathy for what I, and as I soon discovered, thousands of my neighbors and fellow Irving residents, were feeling.

I also knew first hand from my journalism days that city hall can be a cruel stage for mocking earnest, sincere, angry political rookies. I'd seen it before. I'd listened to politicians make fun of upset residents attempting to forcefully express their concern and disgust before such august city councils.

I believed as well, and correctly, that Irving's politicians, aware of this incendiary newspaper article, were already entrenching themselves for the backlash.

This left my future co-conspirators and me a very narrow window of opportunity; a very slim chance for making changes, protecting our neighborhood, protecting our homes, all against a jaded council apparently very comfortable with ignoring their constituents if we allowed them to do so.

At that moment, on that Sunday morning, I and thousands of other Irving residents decided en mass, and independent of each other that being ignored was not an option.

Whether you stay aware of your municipal government and can pick your battles, or wake up under attack as I did, you will soon reach the point where you need to organize your efforts to articulate your demands. And, as happened with me, you will quickly discover you are not the only person feeling what you feel, believing what you believe, and demanding the change it is your right to demand from your government.

Your people are out there. Find them. Gather them. Build on your strength and, most important of all, focus your efforts on what you want to change then keep your focus. That's how you get what you want.

Again, a crucial component, something you must consider before your first meeting, is how to communicate with your group once you start your movement.

As we discussed previously, after deciding to call your troops together, use the Internet, either at home or through free access at your local library, etc., and create a web presence for your revolution on any of the free social networks, Twitter, Facebook, etc.

If you are not web savvy, find someone to help you. Pick a short, succinct name for your movement – *Fairness In City Contracts, Equal Employment For Everyone, Citizens For Better Libraries, Stop Dangerous Overdevelopment, Save Our Downtown Historical District,* and claim your cyberspace.

Twitter allows you to send important issue updates, up to 140 characters per message, to everyone in your revolution subscribing to your tweets; very effective when the political landscape gets complicated, as it will very quickly for your movement.

A social network web page is essential for listing your movement's goals and objectives, as well as providing contact information for new recruits and media when your coup picks up momentum.

A web page allows you to list meeting schedules and clearly, succinctly state your issue and your solution for all to read; much more efficient than repeating your message over and over each time you make a call on your telephone tree.

Most social network web pages also provide space for online comments and discussion, keeping the issues fresh and the interest high among your fellow revolutionaries. Create a central source for all information coming from your movement, a touchstone for your troops, advertising for new recruits, and an identity for your revolution.

Again, if possible, do this before your first meeting so you can alert your fellow revolutionaries of the URL address when you have everyone assembled. We will discuss creating and organizing your revolution's communications efforts a bit later in this book.

The first meeting of your revolution is the most important meeting. You have two immediate objectives: You must proclaim your objective, and you must pick speakers for upcoming assaults on city hall.

But, before you can get to those tasks, ask this question:

"Is everyone here registered to vote?"

This is vital. Among all of the other preparations for your first organizational meeting – alerting people of the meeting's time/location, creating a webpage, etc. - make a trip to your local post office, library, city hall, county/parish office and grab a pile of voter registration applications.

If you must pursue your revolutionary aims to their logical, ultimate extent of electing new representatives, you will need votes to win, all you can get. Voters aligned with your movement. And even if you never have to help elect a slate of candidates as I did, it never hurts to bring more concerned people into the democratic process by registering them to vote.

Make a habit of asking "Everybody here registered to vote?" every chance you get. It is appropriate at almost every meeting you attend, except perhaps before addressing your city council.

But even when making an appearance at city hall, carry registration forms and register everyone you can before and after the meeting. Ballots are the final word in every political decision. Take every opportunity to recruit.

After asking your mandatory voter registration question, call your meeting to order and take charge of your revolution.

Simply, accurately state what brought all of you from the comfort of your homes. Begin with a succinct, high-level statement; why you are meeting; the reason for your distress and anger; the wrong you intend to right; the objective you intend to accomplish. The reason for your revolution.

Short and sweet.

I refer to this as the 50,000 foot statement. Like flying over at altitude, looking down and describing your intention/problem/goal in one short, strong sentence. Your revolution's mission statement.

Something like this:

"We are here tonight to demand more gender-equality in the service contracts awarded by our city as well as fairer municipal hiring practices."

Or:

"We are here tonight to stop the city's destruction of our historical downtown buildings."

Or:

"We are here tonight to save the Smith Park Forrest."

Or:

"We are here tonight to demand more culturally-representative hiring practices for our police force."

Or:

"We are here tonight to demand better, safer libraries."

Or, as in my case:

"We are here tonight to stop the dangerous overdevelopment ruining our city."

If you can explain your objective in a single, simple sentence - a statement people can easily understand, grasp, and readily repeat - you will win.

Conversely, if you cannot reduce your message to a single, simple, motivating statement, your chances of reforming city hall are limited, perhaps fatally.

Think about it. What do you want to accomplish? Be specific. Be direct. Be no bullshit.

The other purpose for your mission statement is to control and focus your movement during your initial meeting. Everyone attending will share strong feelings – if they didn't, they wouldn't be there.

They will agree, applaud, and support what you say. Then, as soon as you finish, each will want to relate their "war stories", the personal, usually passionate impressions and experiences that led them to be part of your rebellion.

Nothing wrong with passion. It gets people up off their asses. But you only have so much time to get your coup moving, and you still have another crucial objective to complete – preparing your presentation, your initial assault on your city government.

Look out over your fledgling revolutionaries; remind them you intend to take your cause down to city hall. To do that successfully, you need volunteer speakers.

While your assembled co-conspirators are certainly more than motivated enough to march on city hall – again, they left the comfort of their homes to attend your meeting - you will find that most people consider the idea of speaking in public, especially on local cable access to a possibly hostile board, commission or city council, somewhat difficult. That's OK. You only really need three or four, and you must choose them wisely.

As you look out over your group, find the three or four persons who best represent different viewpoints that demonstrate broad based support of your cause.

In my case, I looked out over my troops and saw the raised hands of a mother/school teacher, an advertising salesman, an engineering manager for a local airline, and an Episcopal priest. All experienced in some form of public speaking. All able to convincingly press a point verbally. All embodying real-world experience and credibility from different points of view.

You must be able to convince the board/committee/council that you and your movement represent a majority of grounded, logical, sincere voters, stirred from their comfort and silence to seek change.

Again, passion is OK, as long as the message remains logical and sincere. Hence, my harping earlier on the need to effectively present your position at city hall to be taken seriously.

Remember, in many cases, the people you will address are looking for reasons to dismiss you and your movement. Do not give them any reasons.

As a wizened creature of marketing, politics trades largely on demographics; stupid, simplistic, brutal, stereotypical superimposition of easily categorized, easily manipulated patterns on persons perceived to reside in a particular group.

While I do not subscribe to this philosophy, I do recognize that, mostly because of the media saturation of our society and the media's need to reduce us to easily-marketed-to-chunks of humanity, our politicians perceive us as representatives of whatever social group we tend to resemble. They reduce us to symbols, cutouts, whether we as individuals are actually anything like what they think they see or not.

From that dangerous assumption, our politicians presume our wants and needs, along with their rough estimations of our collective intelligence. With these numb, lame assumptions, our elected representatives formulate solutions they believe will best placate us so we'll go away and leave them alone.

Beat them at their own game.

The necessary marketing evil I chose for my coup was to tell our story via our four representatives, knowing that each would easily resonate with my city council from different demographics even the councilpersons could recognize. Like casting reality television for stupid politicians.

Presenting broad based support for your issue and your movement makes it far more difficult for the local officials you encounter to dismiss you as some nut job that enjoys screaming at the council on cable TV.

Instead, you are creating a focused, commonsense presentation from a *group* of people with whom the board/committee/council can easily identify. By spreading your story across several speakers you make it as difficult as possible for your audience of politicians, along with any adversaries lurking in that audience, to categorize and dismiss you.

The other advantage of using demographics against city hall is that the broader your base appears, the more voters it represents in the eyes of the board/committee/council you and your movement are addressing.

This is very powerful, especially when your speakers are backed by 30 or 40 supporters in the audience applauding each point you make.

Most politicians try to estimate the number of voters affected by a particular issue by the number of people attending a meeting to voice their opinion on that issue. Politicians calculate this impact by counting the number of concerned audience members and multiplying by 100.

This is an essential concept.

If you have four or five people making succinct, logical points and each point is passionately applauded by 30 or 40 people in the audience, the committee/board/council members interpret your appearance as representing possibly 3,000 to 4,000 voters!

Leverage.

That many votes, especially angry votes, makes any politician nervous, antsy, uncomfortable, especially if you, your four or five speakers, and your 30 or 40 supporters are making your support of, or opposition to, an issue crystal clear.

Again, reducing anyone to a mere demographic component is terrible, probably one of the most heinous artifacts of our modern culture, certainly with no place at all in our political system.

But as long as we elect politicians who see us a nothing more than some in-the-box, easily categorized, easily appeased, easily dismissed voting cattle, then, as Alexis de Tocqueville said, "we get the government we deserve".

We deserve better, and in planning and staging a successful revolution, we must sometimes embrace a less-than-acceptable status quo in order to replace it. That's working within the system – perhaps the best reason why the system must change.

In the initial meeting of our revolt, our presentation took shape very quickly. Our school teacher/mother could describe the fears she had of the unbearable traffic through our neighborhood, especially how her little children were denied, on a daily basis, access to their playground across an unsafe, traffic-jammed McArthur Blvd. during rush hour.

She could also talk about her professional experience as a 4th grade teacher and the negative impact the constantly shifting student population had on her lesson plan and classroom.

Our airline engineering manager could present a technical, data laden-discussion, strategically using the city-sponsored traffic studies of Valley Ranch, showing the impact additional traffic produced by the proposed overdevelopment would have on the already stressed main boulevard through our neighborhood, especially during rush hour when our teacher/mother was trying to safely move her children across to the playground.

Our Episcopal priest could address the moral inequity of devoting city money and infrastructure to support new, ritzy development in one part of town, when there were so many other sections and neighborhoods crying out for repair and improvement.

Part of his presentation could touch on the environmental impact the overdevelopment would have, especially on the slow-growing Texas live oaks - some of the larger ones over one hundred years old

- always mercilessly knocked down, beaten to death by bulldozers to clear the development acreage.

Our advertising salesman could address the apparent nationwide impression among developers of Irving being an easy place to make a fast, massive fortune, and why that was not really a good reputation to have, especially when those profits came at such a huge cost to Irving residents.

That made me the closer, last in our presentation, reading a list of demands. All the issues we expected the city council to consider and address before they voted on whether to allow the zoning change in question.

I would make sure to touch on every point my fellow revolutionaries made, along with a few other demands of my own, including the need for a citywide tree ordinance prohibiting destruction of any trees four inches or more in diameter.

We had a week, more than enough to hone our message and time our speeches.

Time your speeches - very important. Most city hall meetings, regardless of the board, committee or council, limit the amount of time anyone may speak to three or four minutes. This keeps the meeting moving along, while providing the chairperson a means to stop a speaker who meanders on and on for no particular reason.

In my journalism days, I witnessed on more than one occasion the phenomenon of people angrily droning at the city council for 20 minutes or more about multiple, often completely unrelated issues.

These diatribes could get pretty heated, often ending when the mayor signaled to a police officer, acting as the meeting sergeant at arms, to gently but firmly move the irate speaker off the guest podium and out the door.

Not your problem. Your responsibility in preparing your presentation is to avoid any rambling in any of the speeches you and your fellow revolutionaries give. Meet as often as possible before you assault city hall to practice and make sure your presenters are on the same page, ready to effectively portray your movement's message.

Remain flexible. New ideas, arguments and data will emerge during your preparation. Accommodate them as you need, up to and including drafting additional speakers if a new viewpoint or revelation occurs that helps your story.

Just be mindful that the attention span of your local politicians is pretty short, especially, as in our case, they seemed to have already made up their minds about our issue.

Short, crisp, to-the-point presentations, five or six, max, will serve you best. Get your arguments across in quick, easy-to-remember points. Make them easy-to-quote too. The local press will be listening, and you want as many of your ideas in the next newspaper and on local media as you can get.

You need the press on your side to get what you want. You need them to get behind your revolution. You need them to educate the thousands of readers, the multi-thousands watching the local news on TV, about your issue.

You need the media to take on your cause, to champion your right to participate in the democratic process, to extend you their clout - the power to make many thousands of people aware of what you want, why you want it, and interested in your fight to get it.

The moment you accurately, effectively, passionately articulate your issue, you will attract hundreds of friends you are yet to meet; comrades who will see you on TV, who will read your words, and know you are fighting the good fight, and want to help you win. You also have the benefit of a news media industry that lives to promote the underdog.

Why? It sells newspapers. It makes great television. It gives reporters a story with legs. A story that will go on for awhile, one their audience will want to follow, one that develops to an interesting conclusion.

And, in the interest of larger audiences, the news media will help foment your issue if you provide them with an approachable message, a broad base of support, and articulate people working to bring about a needed change.

Let the media help you. Design your presentation so they have to run with it. Create transcripts of your speeches with bullet points they can copy. Hand your transcripts to reporters. Post them on your web site – AFTER you make your speeches! No use giving your adversaries any advantage by letting the cat out of the bag too early.

Then, in the time before your first presentation, your coup début, practice-practice-practice.

You are about to hit the political stage. Many people are about to hear the first roar of your rebellion. Thousands are about to read your words in the newspaper. Most will be inspired. Some will be angered. Some will turn over to the sports section. No matter. You are about to take your fight downtown to city hall. You are about to become a full-blown activist. *A revolutionary.*

Get ready!

Joe B. Vaughan, Jr.

Communications

As mentioned previously, if possible, prior to conducting your first meeting, create your web presence on Twitter and the other free social networks, such as Facebook, etc. Then, during your initial meeting, after first registering new voters and picking your spokespersons, create a communications committee for your movement.

Your communications committee should consist of a communications manager, someone to write content for your group's page and flyers, along with someone web savvy-enough to take over creation/management of your web presence on Twitter, FaceBook, etc. Again, if your web page is available at your first meeting, you can give your troops the web address(s), and get them to subscribe to the movement Twitter account, saving another round of telephone tree.

Your revolution's webpage need not be anything fancy. It's function is to communicate the issue that spawned your movement, your goals and objectives, provide contacts for new recruits and the media, and, most important, list meeting schedules, especially city meetings where you need your numbers to get the attention of the city board/committee/council.

The telephone tree is an excellent tool for calling together people for the first time. You may also need to use it to announce your web site if you develop it after your initial group meeting. But, as your revolution gains steam, you will find that the telephone tree becomes less effective for communicating with your people.

This is because, as your issue heats up, the people you call will want to vent, turning a 2-minute call into a 20-minute political discussion. Then you have to start all over again with the next call.

Too much to discuss, too little time.

Keep the telephone lists available, especially when you need to remind your movement of important events, such as elections, etc. but charge your communications committee with the care and feeding of your web sites and get back to leading your revolt.

Another excellent low tech tool for alerting the general public to your revolution is using paper flyers. These can be distributed on community bulletin boards, taped to telephone poles, handed out at grocery stores, with permission of course, etc.

Make sure you prominently list your issue, your movement's name, and your web address, all in large, easy-to-read print.

Flyers are harmless enough, although always ask permission before posting/distributing them in any shopping center, business or city facility.

Also, DO NOT place flyers in mailboxes! This violates federal law, and while rarely, subjectively enforced, such violations give your potential adversaries petty ammunition to use against you when your revolution threatens them.

After your initial organizational meeting, work closely with your presentation team. Meet as often as possible to gauge the effectiveness of each presentation, to decide on the order you will follow to optimize the overall impact of your message, and to make sure all your necessary points are being articulated, and within city meeting time constraints.

Another interesting phenomenon I noticed during my movement's first meeting was the appearance of a neighbor who held a seat on both Irving's P&Z, and as a board member of my local homeowner's association.

Spy! I thought. But in the interest of a true, fair revolution, I allowed him in to speak.

He explained with much gravity in his delivery what we were up against: A difficult, nearly impossible uphill battle.

He took a long pause to let his ominous message sink in, arms folded authoritatively, basking in the brief, heavy silence before drawing a storm of angry, savage fire from all quarters around the meeting.

Numerous pointed questions of: "Why aren't you association bastards sticking up for us?", and "What the hell are we paying our dues for if you guys are too chickenshit to do want we need you to do?"

He tried to tap dance through that minefield with the old litigation avoidance argument, but my fellow revolutionaries didn't buy a word of it.

He turned to me, an acknowledgement I suppose of my chairing the meeting, as if to request that I get these yokels back in line. I chuckled, shrugged then nodded towards my front door.

Paranoia was closer than even I anticipated. We were apparently threatening lots of money here, making a fuss over how we wanted our city governed.

I smiled watching him sulk out of my house. The fat cats now knew we weren't rolling over easily, especially if this was the best shot they had to shoot.

It wasn't their best shot. We damned sure weren't rolling over.

Joe B. Vaughan, Jr.

Engagement

Expect an interesting mixture of butterflies and moxie the first time you assault city hall.

Hours before hand, you will find yourself rehearsing your speech in your head, out loud while you drive, in between whispered quips that "it's just city hall" and "*open mic night* with the good ol' boys", but don't kid yourself. This is serious.

The people your will address can be considered amateur politicians only in that most of them do not directly accept pay, or much pay, for what they do.

Make no mistake. Big money is riding on the decisions of the board/commission/council you intend to influence. They don't play.

Your city should be operating to help you, or at the very least, not to cheat or threaten or endanger or harm you in any way. And, if city hall is making decisions that are unfair, prejudicial, corrupt, or without regard to you, your home, your family, your friends, your neighbors, it is your responsibility to change that government.

March down to city hall and serve notice. Rebellion in the house, demands in hand.

No more business as usual.

The first step on this important occasion is signing up to speak. Usually, at any city meeting, there is a signup list near the stack of agendas listing the order items will be discussed in the meeting.

Find your agenda item on the signup list then write your name and address in the appropriate category - either for or against. The mayor or chairperson leading the meeting uses this list to call people from the audience to speak at the guest podium.

When an agenda item comes up in a meeting, the mayor or chairperson announces it by its agenda number then reads the official item description. Sometimes, these descriptions can be very technical and confusing, so if, after reading the agenda, you are uncertain which issue is yours, ask before the meeting begins.

Prior to meetings at city hall, there are always city staffers scurrying around, preparing the panel, exhibits, etc. These are good people. Polite and helpful. Ask them to explain anything on the agenda you may not understand. They will help you. That's their job.

If your presentation is spread across several people and the order each person speaks is important to the overall impact of your presentation, sign up your speakers in the order you want them to speak.

As I mentioned earlier, in the interest of keeping meetings at a manageable length, speakers are usually limited to three or four minutes each. Again, check with your city on actual time allowances.

This is why rehearsing the points you need to make is so important. Either for or against the agenda item, if you can wrap up your message in or under the allotted time; your points are made, your message is delivered, and you stand a much better chance of getting what you want.

Conversely, if you go overtime - especially if you are addressing a hostile board/committee/council - don't be surprised if you are stopped mid-sentence and asked to take your seat.

I've seen it happen many times: A speaker runs long, the crucial, vital point saved for last then left unsaid because the speaker's time runs out. And the more a speaker demands to make that last point, the louder the opposition from the board/committee/council, usually until the official shout down becomes more important and memorable than the argument being made when time ran out.

Practice-practice-practice!

Make sure you can make all your points in the time you are given. If not, edit down your speech to fit the time, or break your speech into two parts and find another speaker to make your additional points for you.

You are there to be heard. You are there to make the arguments that roused you to action in the first place. Make sure you use your opportunity effectively. You may not get another chance.

After the agenda item is announced during the meeting, the chairperson or mayor asks those in favor of the item to speak first. Everyone signed up to speak in favor is allowed to present their argument for why the issue should be supported by the board/committee/council.

The first in-favor speaker is usually the person, or represents the person, who requested the item be added to the agenda. This can be another resident, a board/committee/councilmember, or in the case of a zoning request, the developer or the landowner.

Along with speaking first, this person must also remain available to answer any questions from the board/committee/council members about the agenda item.

Additionally, this initial in-favor speaker is often called back to the guest podium to respond to any points made or questions raised by those opposing the agenda item.

After those speaking in favor are done, those opposing the issue are called in the order they signed up to voice their concerns and make their arguments on why the issue should be denied.

Each speaker opposed to the agenda item may be questioned about the points they make during their presentation by the board/committee/council, but usually, once an opposition speaker finishes, she or he is not called to return to the guest podium.

Again, very important! If you are speaking in opposition, make sure your points are articulated clearly, simply, effectively, because you may not get another opportunity during the meeting to speak on your issue.

Equally important: Like its not-so-distant cousin, the entertainment industry, politics interprets the importance of any issue by the amount of attention that issue attracts; the buzz; the number of people willing to leave their comfortable homes and take to the streets, down to the meeting, into the meeting room or council chamber, interested, involved, agitated, ready.

As I mentioned earlier in this book, politicians, especially city hall politicians hear speeches and presentations and begging and pleading all the time, usually in nearly empty meetings.

As a result, any issue that attracts 30 or 40 residents profoundly impacts the city officials running the meeting.

Again, considering we are talking about politicians, or their board/committee appointees (future politicians), the calculation is usually pretty simple and quick – the number of people there because of an issue multiplied by 100.

That means if you arrive at your meeting with your co-conspirators, and your city officials calculate your numbers as, say, 30, they believe they are addressing an issue resonating across approximately *3000 voters*!

I repeat this important point because most municipal elections and referendums are decided by mere hundreds of votes. For some cities, the sad truth is that most elections attract only a few thousand voters, even though many more people may be registered there to vote.

This makes the good people in the audience supporting you, and the impression they create on the panel you are addressing critically important. Be civil. Be polite. Be courteous and be MANY.

Group manners are important. While you may be facing an insensitive, inflexible, possibly corrupt board/committee/council - and even for local politicians, some of the people you may face can be the most pompous, pretentious, dismissive jerks you will ever encounter - there is no reason for you, your co-conspirators, or your revolution to sink to their level.

Don't do it.

This is especially important for the supporters seated behind you during your presentation. Your opposition may attempt to minimize and discard your legitimate concerns and objections, no matter how eloquently you and your partners articulate them.

In fact, the more eloquent, polished and persuasive you are, the more your opponents may rudely object – a good sign you are winning your discussion!

Those seated behind and around you, there to show their support, should never boo or cat call or respond negatively with anything more than a low grumble, and only then if your opponents are being especially rude.

Politicians are naturally predisposed to dismiss, outright, any discussion with which they disagree when that discussion degenerates into a shouting match. Look at the public forums called by senators and congresspersons to discuss national healthcare.

More often than not, they deteriorated into screaming matches, making great TV, but afterwards each side walked away certain it was absolutely right, the other side was absolutely wrong, that there was absolutely no way to discuss the issue constructively in public, and *nothing was resolved.*

This is what passes today for political discussion in our country.

Fortunately, in local government, we have the opportunity to take our ideas down and present them personally in public forum, directly to our elected officials. Use that opportunity politely and effectively. If your adversaries resort to disturbance or noise, politely ask your council make them behave then finish your statement. You are there to make your point, not suffer selfish dumbasses.

During your meeting with city council, it is your right and well within etiquette for you and your fellow revolutionaries to applaud and show vehement approval of anything said or done with which you agree. That is why you are there.

That is especially why your 30 or 40 supporters are there. You want absolutely no question in your city officials' minds what you want. They must know by the end of your first encounter exactly for what you and your revolution stand, as well as how many good people stand with you.

When you go to your first public presentation, arrive early. Stride proudly to the signup sheet. Sign up your speakers beneath the appropriate agenda item and in the appropriate category, in favor of or in opposition to, and then gather your troops.

Grab an agenda then select seats for your group, easy to see from where your board/committee/council is seated on the panel.

Usually, those in favor of agenda items sit on the left side of the room facing the panel, those opposing agenda items on the right.

In either case, seat your troops where your city officials can easily see their faces and read their expressions. Then, politely, quietly, allow your city government to conduct its business until your agenda item comes up.

When your time comes to speak at the guest podium, addressing your city officials as a speaker for your revolution, take a deep breath. Take more deep breaths and *slow down*.

No, really. Slow down.

You've practiced what your want to say, probably over and over for days in your head. Three or four minutes may have seemed far too brief when you were writing and rehearsing your speech. It is actually plenty of time, especially if you've practiced making your points and you are ready to speak.

The reality is that most people, especially those new to the experience of public speaking, tend to rush through their presentations.

We're talking mach speed here; words spewed at the panel of city officials with machinegun staccato, way too fast to register, especially on any city official predisposed to dismiss your message before you ever get to deliver it.

You have important things to say. Make sure your city officials hear every point you make. Relax, smile, speak distinctly. Look your city officials in the eyes. Thank them for giving you the opportunity to participate in this important discussion. Make your points, regularly looking up from your text and smiling as you speak.

Even if you are delivering serious, important, potentially harsh realities in your message, smile. You are there to make things better. Better for you. Better for your family. Better for your neighbors and friends. Better for your city.

Smile in your good work. And when you complete your presentation, smile again. Thank your city officials and your audience then sit down.

You can do this, and it gets easier the more you do it. We all start from relatively the same point, so smile and tell city hall what you want.

The first time I spoke in front of the Irving City Council, I was completely jazzed on adrenaline, so much so I ripped through my first two demands so quickly the mayor stopped me and asked if I would slow down and state them again.

"The city staff is trying to jot down your points," he chuckled, "and I don't want them to miss anything."

I felt my face flush while I glanced up to see the city secretary and another staff member scribbling frantically on legal pads, trying to keep up with my buzz saw delivery.

One of my presenters whispered "relax" from behind me. I paused, took a deep breath then began again, this time slower, more deliberately. I also stopped between points to allow my troops to applaud and cheer. And they did!

Very important: Always pause to allow applause. Again, this is the opportunity for your supporters to make their presence and sentiments known in this important meeting at city hall. This is their role just as making your speech is your role. Allow your supporters to participate, to voice their support of every point you and your fellow presenters make, and to make sure your city officials are completely aware of the power and depth of your rebellion.

On the night of our first presentation, my speakers and I signed up and then mingled with our supporters, eventually 40 or more of them, as they came in for the meeting. We selected our seats and discussed our issue until the meeting began.

One of the coolest images I remember for our initial assault on city hall occurred just before the meeting was called to order. Several of the councilpersons showed their concern and, in some cases, nervousness across their faces as they scanned my fellow revolutionaries, trying to judge our mood and resolve.

I saw only two smiles on the council during this pre-meeting reconnaissance – more about them later – along with frowns from the other five, and the city manager.

The mayor gaveled the meeting to order then immediately acknowledged our presence, claiming not to know why we were there, but happy to see new faces at the city council meeting.

When our issue came up on the agenda, the requestor, a developer wanting to add another 250 apartment units to Valley Ranch, rose with some very slick graphics and posters, showing architectural drawings of his project.

He was accompanied by his lawyer who reminded the council that there were many uses already allowed in the existing zoning for this property, all far worse than a new apartment complex, making this project the better choice for this land - a very common tactic in zoning cases.

When our turn came to speak, my presenters made their respective points; the impact of multi-family overdevelopment on our neighborhoods, traffic and our schools. The very negative image overdevelopment was making for our city, along with the unethical, unfair application of city resources to benefit one part of the city at the expense of all others.

We used the city-sponsored traffic study data to show how dangerously congested our streets already were, and how bad they would become if Irving continued this dangerous trend of overdevelopment.

Then I rose, and after my rapid-fire miss start, read through my list of demands, including designating any trees, especially the century-old Texas live oaks, with four-inch or larger trunk diameters as protected, untouchable by developer bulldozers.

I demanded a better, more accurate study of the impact of the rush hour traffic on my neighborhood's main boulevard, especially with regard to emergency response.

Finally, I demanded to know how many more apartments, what density per acre, could possibly be built in Irving. I paused with this point then asked it again, looking directly at the city manager. He glanced over at a staff member who shrugged – a very important point I will explain later.

When our presentation was completed, our group stood and applauded. We applauded until the mayor gaveled the meeting back to order. We applauded until the council knew they had a problem on their hands; a large, organized, focused movement prepared to articulate our message to get what we wanted.

There was more discussion from the floor, primarily from the developer's corner offering defense to the points we'd made against his project specifically, and justifying the city's reasoning to allow such projects in general.

"I want to again remind the council that there are several uses allowed in the property's current zoning," he then sneered over at us from the guest podium, "many I believe are far less desirable than apartments."

He went on to list truck stops for 18-wheelers; warehouses, some certified to store hazardous materials; trailer sales and storage lots, requiring huge banks of high powered security flood lights that would glare down over adjacent homes and apartments in our neighborhood.

Each allowable use was worse, and the expressions of horror across most of the faces of the city council perfectly telegraphed the subsequent vote - 5-2 to grant the zoning change, allow 250 more apartments in Valley Ranch.

Each councilperson voting in favor explained they felt the apartments were the "highest and best use of the property", and far superior to any of the terrible projects this developer was threatening to bring about if he didn't get his zoning change.

Several councilpersons chided us for arriving so late to the party. Snippy questions about where we'd been when the zoning change was first requested at P&Z. One councilperson lectured us on participating in what she labeled as a drive-by protest from spoiled homeowners unaware of the difficult, daily work the council had to do to properly govern Irving. That we should all go back and educate ourselves on political etiquette before bothering to interrupt another council meeting.

The two dissenting votes replied, to our applause, that no city should ever be held hostage by a developer threatening to do something dreadful with their property if she or he did not get a desired council decision.

The first dissenting councilperson proposed a thorough review of city zoning specifications to work towards eliminating such adverse uses from the codes.

The second dissenting councilperson thanked us for attending the meeting then made a formal request to add the points we made in our presentation to the next council meeting agenda, especially my demand to know how many more apartments could be built in Irving.

As part of his request, he asked the city manager again if he knew the number, off the top of his head, how many more apartments could ultimately be built in Irving, and at what density – how many units per acre. The city manager replied that he had no way to determine that number – not exactly the response one might expect from the person running one's city.

We soon found out that he was telling the truth. No one in the Irving city government could say with any certainty how many more apartments could be zoned and developed inside our city limits.

The reason no one knew was not bad math skills at city hall, or fear of a riot, or ignorance of the remaining, undeveloped property available inside city limits. The reason was sinister, shocking, and completely political.

But, I'm getting ahead of myself.

We lost our vote. We'd arrived a little late to change a decision probably made weeks or months before most of us were even aware there was an issue - the reason for our revolution.

No matter. There were many votes to come, to be made by local elected officials obviously out of touch with their constituents.

Constituents now awake and aware and watching everything.

Resonance

Things happen fast after you make your first presentation; after you publicly proclaim your intention to your board/commission/council that you want changes in your government and the way it represents you.

People wake up.

Some are astounded because they believed no one else shared their concern with the issues you and your fellow revolutionaries so craftily articulated.

Some will want to join your movement immediately, help any way they can. Others will approach you offering coalitions with their groups to present a united front on a larger variety of issues. Some will want your movement's backing and support and openly court your endorsement.

If you and your co-conspirators have done a good job putting your issue on the map, you will immediately enjoy the principal product of your resonance – that sympathetic vibration that turns all eyes and thoughts towards you and your movement - *political leverage*. Use it very wisely.

The moment you offer a concise, impassioned, approachable, logical argument before your city officials, everyone paying attention – your current and future political allies, along with your current and future political adversaries - will feel the power surge in your direction.

You want to convince any political adversaries that your movement is vast and inclusive of every constituent woman and man in your city. That your cause is so simple, so logical, so right that no one could possible resist it, let alone oppose it.

That drives sitting politicians crazy – just what you want!

Manage it properly. The most important consideration for this heady, wonderful phenomenon is to make sure your buzz, as well as any political alliances it attracts, advances your movement. Period. You aren't in this to lose. Be careful and you won't.

The world is full of political vampires. They seek to latch onto any positive motion they sense. They want to ride along on your energy, hoping to gain via sycophantical association with your ideas, your passion, and then maybe take a little credit for all your hard work and time and courage - don't let them.

Political association is necessary. Your movement needs many, many friends; a long line of people wanting to meet with you and gain by that association.

Just make sure you check the background and motivation of anyone, especially anyone apparently powerful, seeking your favor. Find out who they are. Find out who their friends are. If they are elected officials, find out how they've voted on issues similar to yours.

If they represent a group seeking coalition, see what issues they've pushed in the past. See who does their leg work. See what candidates they've previously endorsed. See who pays their expenses, who provides them information, who benefits from their victories.

Amazingly, the first thing your adversaries may try to do is recruit you to blunt your movement. Some will approach you dangling insider status and associations with movers and shakers behind your local government – the same people who created the issue you seek to change with your rebellion.

Rubbing elbows with the local power elite can be extremely intoxicating; like being invited to sit at the "cool kids" table for lunch back in high school.

Say no.

If you weren't already effectively rocking the boat, the local elite wouldn't be bothering with you at all. The infuriating part is that, in making such an offer, they assume you and your co-conspirators are so green, so politically naïve, so stupid that you will be swayed to their side. That's an easy assumption for them to make considering it's probably worked on almost everyone they've used it on so far.

Not this time.

Stick to your guns. Politely consider all offers, but let some time pass before you declare allegiance to anyone. Remember, you and your fellow revolutionaries attracted this attention by being yourselves. By speaking your minds. And now that you have rattled some political cages, sit back and see who wants to play.

The first thing I noticed after we completed our first assault on city hall was several calls from councilpersons, especially the one that lectured us about learning the political etiquette necessary to be effective in public, each offering to take us under her or his political wing. They said they were each making the offer as a concerned individual to mentor and guide us through the treacherous local political waters.

I found out later that each of them had called my other presenters, called in exactly the same order, called offering access to the secretive inner workings of local politics, called asking who was running our movement.

Stupid bastards.

Prior to our presentation, I alerted my group that such offers would certainly come our way. I'd seen it before as a city hall reporter. We agreed that we would listen politely to all inquiries, but wait to exercise our option to associate with anyone until we decided what best suited our collective goal.

Most of our initial suitors didn't like our hesitance very much. They expected us to be so flattered, especially after such stern rebukes at the council meeting that we would roll over for them immediately.

But there were far better offers ahead. They arrived with calls from the two dissenting councilpersons, each seeking to fill us in on what we were up against and who we were threatening.

I again urged caution. Just because they voted in our favor on an obviously long ago-decided zoning issue didn't mean these two were automatically working for the same cause we were. We listened politely but reserved the right to align with either of them until we could meet face-to-face.

I was immediately invited down to the law office of the dissenting councilperson who, like me, questioned the city manager about the number of apartments that could ultimately be built in Irving. He greeted me with a several-inches-thick stack of all the proposed multi-family zoning requests in the pipeline for consideration by P&Z.

"I'm not trying to court you," he smiled. "I'm trying to arm you. These are the requests that newspaper article was talking about, along with a bunch more filed *since* the article appeared. This is what's coming in the next 6 months unless you and your associates start raising hell!"

OK. We *were* talking about the same thing.

"If you think things are bad now," he continued, "just wait until all of this bullshit gets approved. At least you can get into the loop early enough to maybe influence P&Z before they rubberstamp all this for the council."

I thanked him and said we would be in touch. I also asked if the other dissenting councilperson at the meeting could be trusted.

"My colleague is running for mayor this spring," he replied. "He hates what's happening and is hoping to find four other candidates to run with him to create a majority bloc on the council to stop the overdevelopment. I'm running for one of those seats. I hope you and your group will agree, that's what needs to happen."

I still wasn't sure how much we should trust anyone besides ourselves at this point of the revolution, but here was some crucial ammunition listing each requested zoning change and when P&Z was scheduled to consider it. Now we could effectively adjust our tactics and arguments for each case. We could participate *very* early in the process, just as we'd been admonished to do during our first city council meeting by one of the sitting councilpersons, soon to announce she was seeking reelection to her seat.

We'd see about that.

I took the documents back to my people and we planned our next assault, the P&Z meeting scheduled the following week. There were three more multi-family zoning change requests scheduled and we decided to restage our presentation as opposition to all three.

A few days before the P&Z meeting, two other groups of concerned Irving residents contacted us independently about forming a coalition. Each group had their own issues.

The first consisted of homeowners in central Irving concerned about the concentration of city resources and new infrastructure on north Irving, including Valley Ranch, to keep that part of town attracting developers at the expense of the rest of the city.

The second group turned out to be a thinly-disguised election campaign for a local real estate agent; a political rival of a sitting councilperson. We discovered the two local politicians had traded council seats back and forth for the previous 10 years, and the candidate on the outside was looking for some fresh muscle.

We politely but firmly told the second group that we were working to change the local political system that, over the past 10 years, had allowed, if not exacerbated the current crisis we opposed. They responded that their candidate saw the error of his ways and would work with us to fix things.

We declined.

Again, you are in this to get what you want. *To win*. Winning means breaking the destructive cycle of "business as usual". If someone approaches your movement, their history, their background and motivations are fair game. Check them out. If they are looking to capitalize on your energy, political vampires looking to feed on your buzz, say no.

We invited the first group to join us at P&Z. We told them we agreed that the deviation of city funds and resources to our end of town was a major injustice to anyone living elsewhere in the city, ignored and deprived of essential municipal services. If we could show city-wide opposition to the zoning changes allowing more overdevelopment, primarily in the northern end of town, we stood a better chance of getting city hall to change its priorities.

On the evening of the P&Z meeting, we arrived with a combined group of 60 people; so many that the P&Z chairperson immediately adjourned the commission into *executive session*, a closed meeting, allegedly to discuss potential litigation, legal under the *Texas Open Meetings Act* after a public meeting is convened.

Check for similar meeting laws used by your state then learn these laws. You would be amazed what some people try to get away with at supposedly public meetings; meetings where it is your right to know about every issue under discussion, along with any decisions made there by your representatives.

Apparently the zoning change applicants, realizing we were coming, threatened a law suit against the city if they didn't get what they wanted. At the time we didn't know how exactly many of our P&Z commissioners were actually in cahoots with developers and property owners.

We found out later that several P&Z board members were also either local real estate agents or, in some way, associated with the development community and local homeowner's associations, including, as we already knew, the aforementioned crasher of our first meeting - the guy that tried to explain our homeowner's association's inability to represent us before city council because of the legal exposure they might incur, and why we were fighting a very difficult, uphill battle.

While there may have been major discussions of the legal consequences of voting to appease the seething coalition in the P&Z audience, I suspect the real reason for the executive session was far more basic and tactical.

The P&Z commissioners wanted to wait us out. Keep the meeting going late so that most of us would grow bored and go home without a fight. Then they could reconvene later before a mostly empty room – only the developers there at that point – and do some more business as usual.

But we stayed.

We did better than that. I called a meeting between the two groups - we had a nice meeting room we were paying for with our property taxes, right? – and we mapped out our agenda as a coalition with full knowledge of the developers sitting on the other side of the room.

I wanted them to know we were serious. We were organized. Sophisticated. Prepared. Aware of our rights. The same rights from which they had no defense.

No more business as usual.

P&Z came back after an hour-and-a-half, some of the members shocked to see most of the coalition still sitting there, ready. Our issues came up and we argued our side.

For our efforts, we got negative recommendations – no zoning change to multi-family - on two of the requests, sending the developers into rage. We lost the third zoning request, approved by a narrow margin. Unacceptable to us, but the city council would still have to vote on all three, so we still had a chance to win that one too, and more work to do.

Equally important, the Irving power structure was now very much aware that there was a new component in the local political process; a radical element apparently prepared to do more than usual to get results. Watching the nervous eyes of the P&Z commissioners, I smiled.

I hadn't expected to encounter such a disorganized, almost frightened reaction. While I knew we'd done our homework, I couldn't help but think a large portion of the shock we were evoking was because the establishment – especially these public servants working so hard for the fat bastards making all the money – wasn't prepared for our numbers and our passionately articulated objections. The fact was that they weren't prepared for any resistance at all.

Our city government was really just a development greed party made possible by the apathy of Irving residents; the same residents paying the freight while being excluded from the guest list.

After so many years, unchecked greed evolved the legally-required public meetings, discussions, ruminations and votes to poorly attended, dimly lighted, murky coronations.

Prostrate developers feigning humility, submissively shuddering in character just long enough to receive a light tap on each shoulder from the mayor's money wand then rising from the council chamber carpet, clutching large shiny briefcases, loping off, money giddy, to larger, shiner cars, leaving a dark muculent stain behind in our city hall for the rest of us.

Not much longer.

Joe B. Vaughan, Jr.

Protraction

The other interesting thing that occurs in any successful political movement is the broadening of goals. After you mount your successful initial assaults on your local government, the full extent of the problem you are fighting to change tends to reveal itself, a little here, more there, until you begin to get the full picture.

Where previously you may have sought a simple resolution to your issue, you may now see that the system that allowed the problem to occur in the first place requires a significant overhaul.

Joe B. Vaughan, Jr.

This is not to say that movements successfully resolving single significant problems are not as important, as necessary, as justified as full scale system-corrections, not at all.

In fact, if more people got involved in our political process at every level, each of us might be afforded the luxury of holding watch over smaller pieces, knowing that every other facet of the entire governmental animal was being held responsible by other interested people just like us, invested in making our representative government truly representative.

Rarely the case, unfortunately, and when revolutionaries begin to gain perspective through involvement they realize how much of the system really is rotten, how much work is actually required to first win significant positive changes and then make sure those changes stick.

Because of this, a movement that begins small often turns into a full scale political campaign once the participants realize that their government requires more repair than can be accomplished by fighting for one issue.

This is when talk between your movement and your allies begins to include electing new representation to city hall. Hence my urgings to register new voters at every opportunity.

Broadening goals to include voting political opponents off city council is a natural and expected evolution of your rebellion.

Begin by examining the voting records of the sitting councilpersons in your municipal government considering reelection. Determine who has voted for issues you support, and who has not. If you believe any of your current council members can be trusted, interview them; explain your issue and ask them what they intend to do to resolve it.

Make plans to replace anyone who does not satisfactorily pass your scrutiny. Take no prisoners. Canvass your movement, your friends, your neighbors, your coalition to develop a list of suitable, potential candidates to replace inferior sitting councilpersons.

Usually, as election season approaches, anyone considering a run for a political seat will make her or his presence known by requesting a meeting to court your support.

As with all previous phases of your growing revolution, be courteous, but be careful. The candidates you endorse must understand why you took to the streets in the first place, and that you make no endorsements lightly. You *expect* whoever you elect to make your demands law.

Any candidate unable to guarantee that your issue is her or his top priority, the first thing she or he will bring up after swearing in on council, is not worth your time. Remember, if you weren't creating significant resonance with your movement, no one would be seeking your support. You have the leverage – use it.

You may also begin to hear suggestions that you and/or your co-conspirators run for election. If you want to participate on that level and you have the time and inclination, consider the offer. Again, if more people participated in all facets of our political system, it would behave with much more compassion and logic.

The bottom line is that participation, either as a candidate or as an activist is what we seek; the essential element that, for the most part, is rare or missing completely in all forms of American government today. And, if each of us, in our own capacity, take the time to make sure our governments are working as they should, we all benefit, and by far less effort than my fellow revolutionaries and I were forced to expend to correct the seriously corrupt, broken system in our city.

After time and meetings and consideration and more meetings, carefully select your candidates then make the world aware of your endorsements. Use your web page. Use the media. Call a joint press conference with your coalition and announce your candidates for each seat, and why they are your candidates. Leave no doubt who you like, and what you expect.

Next, take every opportunity to demonstrate the differences between your endorsed candidates, your slate, and their opponents. Sponsor debates. Invite all candidates for each seat then ask them to address your issues. They're *your* debates, right? If opposition candidates refuse to participate, ask why. Ask why in the media!

Also, seek to contribute to any other debates planned around your city. Most political event organizers appreciate any help they can get, including preparing questions for the candidates. And, with all your movement's hard work articulating your viewpoint and issues, your participation will likely be sought to validate the event, if not to keep things lively.

Again, be polite and focused, but take the opportunity to make the difference between your candidates and their opponents obvious and easy to understand. Simply ask each candidate if she or he supports your side in the question; if so, what do they plan to do to bring about the change you demand; if not, why not.

In my case, a surge of meeting invitations for my fellow revolutionaries and me began after the two councilpersons supporting our issue announced for reelection, one of them now running for mayor. Both stated support or our issue, as well as issues identified by other allied movements around Irving, and that they were seeking our endorsement for their campaigns.

We were becoming important fixtures in the local political environment, even invited to meetings with our adversaries, the most interesting being one developer with whom we met privately where he begged us to back off our opposition to his zoning request, promising that if we allowed him to make his profit, he'd take the money and leave Irving, never to develop here again.

We turned him down flat. He responded that he expected as much, denouncing us at a subsequent council meeting because we were so difficult to work with, and that the city should pay us no more attention because we were just a pack of self-indulgent homeowners trying to keep an honest man from making a living.

The council, aware that development questions were becoming major political ammunition for our candidates, tabled the zoning change, prompting an enraged rant from the developer including threats to sue the city for impeding his success.

Think about that for a moment.

Here was a person seeking approval to make a boatload of cash, only able to make that boatload if the council gave him permission.

Now he was threatening that very body of city officials, as well as every resident in the city, with a lawsuit if he didn't get his way, thinking that, via his scary lawyers, satiating his greed was more important than the wishes of all of the voters who elected the city council to represent them.

Evil bastard.

The coalition formed by my movement and others around the city participated in several debates, one in which I got to question the candidates, focusing on our issue of overdevelopment in Irving. The responses were very telling. Opposition candidates raised the specter of endless law suits if a newly elected council dared resist the developers drooling to carve up what was left of our city.

It sounded like a rehearsed response, almost word-for-word, each opposition candidate showing a worried scrunch across her or his brow, moaning fears of the future legal battlefield Irving would become if things were not allowed to continue just the way they were.

Yeah, right.

Our candidate for mayor countered that Irving had a city attorney, hired explicitly to defend our city and its residents from any legal threat. He pledged that if elected mayor, he would command the city attorney to aggressively take on any legal challenge from any developer, and that if the current city attorney was afraid to do the job, he would hire a new city attorney who could.

I scanned the shocked faces of the opposition candidates as the audience rose to their feet in applause; a decisive moment where our enemies began to fade a bit, droop their heads, reply to all subsequent questions in carefully worded monotone.

That moment was eclipsed by the absolute showstopper delivered by our other councilperson seeking reelection; the lawyer who presented me with the huge stack of zoning requests in the pipeline for P&Z consideration. He told us that, during his research to prepare for the debate, he discovered why no one in our city government could answer the question "How much more multifamily development is possible for Irving? How many more apartment units can be built here?"

The answer he discovered was astounding.

Every city projects, designs and builds its future based upon its comprehensive plan. A comprehensive plan usually covers the following five to ten years of a city's future, and is used as a blueprint to manage municipal growth to ensure city services will be adequate and affordable over that period.

To make such predictions as accurate as possible, a comprehensive plan must incorporate the ratio of single family development to multifamily development. Stipulating this ratio allows city planners to properly predict and control how and where the city will grow, what the population will probably be, and where city infrastructure and services should be focused.

A healthy ratio for any city is usually 90% single family to 10% multifamily, again because a larger percentage of single family development indicates a more predictable population density over the projected life of the comprehensive plan.

Our candidate rocked the debate with his revelation that the reason no one on the city staff could tell us how much more overdevelopment might occur was because no one knew what our single family to multifamily ratio actually was. That was because *Irving had no comprehensive plan*.

While the opposition candidates, many of them sitting councilpersons gasped, our candidate continued to say that Irving had drafted a plan in the late 1960s, but the plan was never approved by the then city council.

No comprehensive plan. Multifamily development in Irving had continued without any master blueprint or guidance or limitations for over 20 years. Our ratio was probably closer to 10% single family to 90% multifamily!

No wonder there were apartments everywhere. No wonder traffic was so screwed. No wonder there was little opposition to more overdevelopment at city hall. Even if someone wanted to stop it, there was no municipal law to set a maximum limit on that development. No law in place to say enough is enough.

None.

This was and remains a technical issue, especially when attempting to explain the importance of a comprehensive plan. Fortunately for me and my fellow revolutionaries, all it took to articulate our problem was to ask voters to look around at the traffic, the overdevelopment, all of the crumbling apartments, some of the older ones now flipped many, many times and deteriorating dramatically.

The clincher at the debate was that all five candidates on our slate pledged to place a moratorium on any multifamily zoning until after a new comprehensive plan was drafted and approved for the City of Irving.

The lead time for writing and approving a new plan was projected to be at least one-a-one-half years. At the minimum, a year and a half where zoning requests to continue the overdevelopment plaguing our city would be tabled until the council got a handle on the actual ratio, and how to best provide adequate city services for current and future residents.

Our sitting opponents were stuck because approving any zoning requests at this point indicated where they stood on overdevelopment, especially after the comprehensive plan debacle.

But, some of them approved certain requests anyway, saying that they were considering each request individually, and that the ones that didn't seem to harm the city were probably alright. More like "Things are already such a mess, how much would a little more here and there actually hurt?"

No matter. Sides were chosen and a low rumble was beginning to permeate every political notion in our city.

The media was aware too. A local television station called two of my speakers and me to a Valley Ranch apartment development site where an entire hillside of fine Texas live oaks had been bulldozed to the ground. The developer had made a point of killing all of these beautiful trees a few days after our triumphant debate.

The TV remote crew videoed us standing in a crater full of broken, dying live oaks, the latest, most apparent casualties of greed, dishonesty and insouciance. An angry statement to bring this war right to our front doors.

Yup. It was war alright. And, as I watched the television camera scan the shattered live oaks, scraped into large piles to burn the following day, a war I knew we were going to win.

The story was broadcast at 6PM and we made sure to mention that the election was only weeks away and that we were backing candidates who wanted to protect our trees and our neighborhoods.

We'd finish this at the ballot box.

Joe B. Vaughan, Jr.

Revolution

In Texas, municipal elections are held on the May uniform election date, the second Saturday in May. Check the Internet to see when your local elections are scheduled each year.

If your revolt requires taking control of a city government, like mine did, you need plenty of lead time before the election to push your issue, pick your candidates, show the public why they should back your movement.

Register new voters too!

Voter registration involves completing a registration form - voter name, address, age, etc. – then mailing the completed registration form back to your county/parish registrar before the registration deadline, usually a month before Election Day.

Postage on these forms is free, and the registration forms are available in various county/parish office locations, post offices, libraries, city hall and online.

Usually, the registration forms are preaddressed for return to your county/parish registrar, but if you receive blank registration forms, fill in the appropriate county/parish registrar address prior to heading to the street to sign up new voters.

Do not wait until 30 days before your election to begin registering voters. Alerting the voting public to your important, passionate issues is useless if you don't have the numbers you need at the polls on Election Day.

Start early! When you decide to form your movement, grab a stack of voter registration forms and get people registered to vote. Make this part of everything you do, every appearance you make, every event you attend; the thing you say before you begin meetings or speeches.

"Before we get started, is everyone here registered to vote?"

Anyone not registered is a potential supporter, first of all because you are helping them embrace the democratic political process, and you are inviting their participation by ensuring their right to vote.

Take the opportunity to introduce yourself as you help them fill out the registration form. Present them with your flyer showing your issues, your candidates, your web site, and other important contact information, and especially the date of the election.

After completing the registration with your new voter, offer to mail the form for her or him; the number of completed registration forms that never get mailed, and would-be voters who never vote exceeds gazillions.

Don't lose a single vote. Make this effortless for new voters. After an appearance at a political event, or a Saturday morning registering voters in front of the local grocery store, with permission of course, take your healthy stack of registration cards to the post office and slip them into the mail slot.

Usually, a voter receives her or his registration certificate from the county/parish registrar in about 30 days. This is a card displaying the voter's name, address, as well as the legislative or congressional district in which the voter lives. Based on the district, the voter can determine via newspaper or Internet, her or his polling place. A list of districts and corresponding polling places in your city is also very helpful addition to your web site and flyers.

As Election Day nears, one would think that keeping people focused and ready would be easy, and generally interest will remain high.

But do not relax. Keep talking and calling and keep your fellow revolutionaries calling, reminding everyone they know, everyone they see, that the election is in a week, a few days, tomorrow, and what is at stake in this important decision they are helping make.

There is another important phenomenon associated with people deciding whether or not to take the time to go to the polls. Sometimes, the margin on an issue, the difference between votes for or against, is far closer than people perceive, making each vote crucial.

We have become amazingly dependent on the questionable accuracy of political polling in this country, a practice that implies huge significance to tiny opinion samples - usually only 1000 people for most national opinion polls. Not necessarily the most trustworthy method of predicting anything, yet most people believe what the polls indicate is reality – even local polls. But never believe anything until the votes are counted. That's what Harry Truman did.

Sometimes an issue that looks like a loser a few days out from an election can actually be won. The margin may be razor thin, but a win is a win, and getting even 50 people to the polls that hadn't planned to be there, or had forgotten when the election was scheduled, makes all the difference.

Even more amazing, sometimes, if an election seems completely certain, voters will decide that there will probably be more than enough support, so they don't need to bother voting.

Always remember, most municipal elections are decided by well within 1000 votes. A vast majority of municipal political decisions are made by only hundreds of votes; some by less than 50 votes.

With numbers like that, you can never stop haranguing your people to go haranguing other people to get to the polls. This is the time to use Twitter and go back to your telephone tree; the list of contacts you've collected throughout your revolution.

Assign 20 names to each or your troops and make sure they call the night before the election to remind people to vote. Be courteous and positive, but make sure the people you call understand how important it is for them to participate in this vital democratic process.

If people need to know where to vote, tell them. If people need to better understand the issues, explain for them. If they need a ride to the polls, go by and pick them up.

It is absolutely, exactly that important.

On Election Day, arrive at your polling place early and vote. Then take your place out past the electioneering limit, indicated by an official marker, normally 100 feet from the polling place entrance. Stand among the other *electioneers*, another title you now own along with activist and revolutionary.

Some of the other electioneers will be friends. Some will be adversaries. Some will be there for other political issues all together. Keep it friendly. Stay polite. Stay focused.

You are not on station to fight or argue. You are there to influence anyone strolling up to the polls who may not have completely made up their minds, may not be aware of your issue, may need more information to make their last minute, informed decision.

The trick is making your pitch earlier, and in a more attractive way, than any adversaries standing next to you, trying to do exactly the same thing. Back to your 50,000 foot statement, the one you used to call your initial revolutionary meeting to order.

Clearly, cleanly, loudly, articulate your issue in as few words as possible to get approaching voters to stop and read your flyer, consider your position, see your list of candidates, ask any questions they may have before they head to the ballot box.

If there is more than one entrance to the polling place, make sure you have people electioneering there, all working in the same friendly, informative manner, guiding people to vote the right way. Your way.

If there is trouble, back out of the conflict and get the attention of any police personnel stationed nearby. Usually, especially in hotly contested elections, there will be police representation, or some other official from the city at each polling place, as well as poll watchers and media. If an adversary tries to make things personal, let the officials handle it.

Sometimes fights are staged to cast some last minute shadows over a movement and the people who support that movement. Do not be drawn in.

You have come too far, learned too much, worked too hard for anything other than that most sublime moment of knowing you have politically kicked your adversaries' asses. Don't mar that with any Election Day physical combat.

Remember that anyone who gets angry enough to make a complete ass of herself or himself, especially on Election Day, especially in public in front of the polls, is losing the election.

That is not you.

Be gracious. Be friendly. Be polite. And enjoy the fact that you are fighting the good fight and that people walking up are supporting you, your movement and all your good work. Work through the day then when the polls close, head to city hall for the results.

This is a wonderful experience. This is American politics in it most genuine form. You and hundreds of other people participating in democracy, all waiting for the city secretary to announce the winners. All waiting for the numbers.

The interesting thing is that there, gathered with your allies and friends, along with adversaries and enemies, the room seems to buzz with conversations all having nothing to do with the election and the months invested by everyone to bring about this important decision. Everyone takes a break, parks the issues, and waits to see what the future of your city is going to look like.

Don't miss it.

On Election Day in my revolution, I got to the polls, my local fire station, the one that was landlocked during the daily rush hours, just after they opened. I voted for my five candidates then took my place on the sidewalk past the electioneering boundary. I had a pile of flyers listing our candidates, along with a short, succinct message to bark at voters walking up.

"Stop over-development! Stop the dangerous traffic jams!"

Worked every time.

People who were trying to stay out of immediate conversation range of me and the 10 or so other electioneers beside me would turn and walk straight to my outstretched hand, take my flyer, my list of candidates then tell me they too were tired of our city being such an overdeveloped mess.

A person to my left, working for one of the sitting councilpersons my group was trying to oust, attempted to keep up with me for the first hour or so.

He then fell silent realizing that there was no way to quickly, effectively explain why anyone should vote for his candidate when I was offering a choice dedicated to resolving our obvious, dangerous problems.

Early in the afternoon, most of my adversaries had abandoned their stations after experiencing an embarrassing five- or six-to-one ratio of people seeking my political advice over theirs. I stayed at my post. Again, municipal elections, even ones apparently going so smoothly, are dynamic and unpredictable, right to the end.

An hour before the polls closed, a member of one of our affiliate groups stopped by to report that she had experienced about the same level of voter support over in her end of town. She'd stopped at the other polling places too and all except one seemed to be decidedly in our corner.

I thanked her for the news, but told her that I'd seen a few of these contests before, and I wanted to make sure I got every vote I could get. She laughed and called me hard core.

Yeah, pretty much.

I watched the polls close then drove to city hall. I joined a sizable group of people standing inside the city council chamber, spilling out into the lobby. Projection screens listed the candidates for each seat; all vote tallies set to zero. The room and lobby were quiet, quieter than I expected, especially after the debates and meetings and all the interest of the past several months; little pockets of people talking about what they wanted to get back to in their lives after the election.

I hadn't thought about that at all until that moment. This politics stuff does take up lots of time. I was attending several meetings each week, and not being a meeting person, way more than I ever imagined I would.

When asked, I responded that after the election I was going to stay as active as necessary to make sure all the things we'd worked so hard to bring about actually happened. I received nods all around I interpreted to mean my co-conspirators, many now my good friends, would be there with me, making sure.

The last ballot boxes arrived and disappeared into the city secretary's office. It wouldn't be long now, we thought.

Actually, it does take a little while to count ballots, especially when, as we soon found out, turnout this election was almost 40% higher than previous years. We'd done our job, gotten the word out, made people aware that they could do something about their city, about their politicians, about their government. We'd had a very good issue, one nobody could argue against, easy to sell. But we'd decided to wake up and make sure we were going to get the change we deserved.

Two hours later, the projection screens flickered then the room erupted with applause. By significant margins, the closest being two-to-one, each of our candidates, our entire slate, was elected. We now owned a five-to-two majority on the council, including the mayor.

We won.

The freshly reelected lawyer that gave me the pile of zoning request notices back at the beginning or our adventure, took me aside, shook my hand then demanded my comrades and I be in the front row of the council meeting the following Tuesday; the meeting where our slate would be sworn in.

"The meeting where I will propose the zoning moratorium," he smiled, shaking my hand again, "to remain in place until we write and approve a new municipal comprehensive plan! Twenty years is just too long."

We were all there the following Tuesday watching each or our candidates be sworn in, our new mayor first, followed by the remaining four of our majority bloc.

First order of business was to propose a new comprehensive plan for Irving accompanied by a moratorium on any new multifamily zoning until the new plan was written and approved. The new council voted the motion into law, unanimously.

We stood and applauded for what seemed like an hour, our candidates, now sworn in councilpersons – *our representatives* - standing and applauding with us.

I can still hear it, even today.

Joe B. Vaughan, Jr.

Aftermath

Victory rocks. It changes everything. When you make your local government accountable to you and your neighbors and your friends, good things begin to happen. Problems that previously went ignored, problems you maybe learned to live with, or at least learned to ignore to get by, begin to change. Things begin to get better.

The change may be dramatic, or it may take a little time. But the amazing thing is that afterwards you will find yourself wondering why you put up with any bullshit at all, when all that was necessary was for people who *could* do something about a problem, *to do something about the problem.*

Enjoy the heady rush of your victory. You earned it. You worked to make a positive change, to make your government accountable to you, your neighbors, your friends and thousands of other people you may never even meet.

Remember this fundamental truth: *A repaired government does not stay repaired on its own.*

Remain vigilant. The more you stay motivated, involved, active, watchful, willing to make your voice heard, the more difficult it will be for your government, your elected representatives, to slip back into the ugly mess you and your movement have worked so hard, given so much of your time to fix.

As I mentioned earlier, if everyone in your revolution takes a piece of your government to watch, a part of the city hall machinery to keep responsive and honest then only minor adjustments are required, especially after a major overhaul.

If you and your troops remain active, especially at reminding your elected representatives that they once had to audition to gain your support - that you can start holding new auditions tomorrow if necessary – you will be amazed at how responsive they are, seeking the people's opinions on important issues, making sure that they still deserve the trust and responsibility your gave them in the election.

While victory is still sweet and the applause still rings in your ears, decide what else needs to be fixed. Then assign your revolutionaries each a piece of the action to manage. Remember, you have the votes and influence on the council now. *Use them.*

That means diversification. That means sending a whole new batch of faces down to city hall, to the boards and committees and council to speak on your behalf.

Some of your troops and you may be offered positions on city committees and boards. If there is something you want to do on this advisory level - for example, champion city sponsorship for care and feeding of the homeless, or advising council on keeping gender-equality a priority in service contract awards - go for it.

Anything to stay in the political grapevine and to make sure that everyone down at city hall knows you and your co-conspirators are still listening.

No secrets. No surprises.

Joe B. Vaughan, Jr.

But again, diversification, for two important reasons. First, as I discovered rolling up to the election, I was spending almost every moment away from my job at meetings, working to make the changes, making speeches, recruiting troops, signing up new voters. I wasn't the only one. There were hundreds just like me.

But the job of making government accountable is far too large for one or two or one hundred people to do. If more people are involved, again more eyes and ears in the various decision loops, then we all get more representation from our government at far less time and sacrifice than if only a few of us take on this very heavy job.

More eyes and ears mean less is missed. Less opportunity for anyone - especially the politicians that promised to always do right - to shirk their responsibilities. And again, if our elected officials get into politics for any other reason than to serve us, we need to know as soon as possible, and boot their lying asses out.

The second reason you have to divide up ownership of your government to as many fellow revolutionaries as possible gets back to what I mentioned earlier about politicians labeling people; making unwarranted assumptions about their constituents because of the way they look or speak or the clothes they wear. In this case, the labeling occurs not because of unfamiliarity, but for exactly the opposite reasons.

If, in your political activism, you continue to voice your opinion before your council all by yourself, or with a dwindling band of followers behind you, you will begin to see the politicians your elected paying less and less attention to what you say.

This is a real problem, especially because of the irritation threshold phenomenon we discussed earlier – the flashpoint issue that gets you and hundreds or thousands of your neighbors and friends on their feet and down at city hall raising hell.

The reverse side of the irritation threshold is that once a political resolution is won, most people no longer feel threatened. They no longer feel irritated. They want to stay home and enjoy their families and rest from work and watch television and do any of the millions of wonderful things that do not include going to city hall and attending meetings.

Duh.

Except that politicians, even the ones you worked so hard to elect, know that sooner or later, interest will lag, and business as usual will creep back in once again.

And then, if you are left with a handful of fellow revolutionaries down battling city hall, you will find your elected representatives paying less and less attention to you.

This is the phenomenon of *overexposure*. It occurs when politicians, even the ones you bring to power, see you standing before them too often. You have the right to appear at every council meeting, explain why your city should be addressing each of the countless other issues that should be corrected to ensure the people get the city services they deserve.

But the more you appear on your own, the more your harangue, the less the politicians seem to hear. Terrible but completely true.

The only cure is keeping so many people involved that city hall cannot focus on any one particular person. Instead, you need to keep your politicians off balance, guessing about the motivations behind anyone standing before them, wondering what the consequences might be for not doing the job they were elected to do.

You *must* keep new faces coming at them all the time.

In my case, the major revelation prior to the election that Irving had been operating without a comprehensive plan for more than 20 years shocked almost everyone, especially as each of us looked around town and saw the result of little or no planning, and the endless scars left behind for us by greedy bastards, some of whom had violated our city over and over again.

The news that our local government would finally step up and stop this destructive process relieved everybody, and many of my fellow revolutionaries called our adventure a good day's work, hung up their political hats, and retired.

I couldn't blame them. After the election I was still involved in trying to make sure the city was aware that there were neighborhoods long neglected and badly in need of city services, along with all the other obvious infrastructural inequities the greedy bastards left behind in their wake.

I was moderately successful, but as my supporters backed away from the process, I found that my speeches carried less and less influence, eventually met with bored stares from *my* councilpersons, as if to say "You're up here again?"

Overexposure.

Hell yes, I was up there again! I was trying to make sure that the apathy that allowed a major American city to go development crazy for over 20 years was not allowed to take root again.

But, without the irritation threshold, explaining increasingly complex political issues to neighbors and friends took longer and longer and the fight to keep our council focused on the issues we thought so important was soon far more than the few of us still involved could do.

We tried. Learn from us. *Keep your revolution focused and involved.*

I also found myself invited to planning meetings with the last few multifamily development projects approved before the moratorium.

Apparently, the developers, fearing any political backlash, felt that having me attend their meetings would gain them some special consideration from the new council. Maybe me being there would be interpreted as some sort of passive approval.

I did not approve. I attended the meetings and suggested the developers give back the acreage they planned to develop, especially if they'd made money previously, developing some of the other atrocities with which Irving residents were forced to live. I told these developers they owed the people of Irving restitution.

They didn't bite. I didn't really expect them to. Their days were pretty much numbered because of the moratorium, and because by the mid-90s, there was no more than about 5% of Irving's landmass still left undeveloped. The only option left them in that scenario was to develop whatever they had zoning for prior to the revolution, or consider reclaiming previously developed multifamily acreage, knocking down the old and building new.

That is actually happening today in some parts of Irving, where the city's central location between Dallas and Ft. Worth remains ideal for commuters.

But, the past is taking its toll on Irving. The city still struggles with the previous misdirection of priorities, the destructive disconnect between what the politicians in control for so long wanted for the city, and what Irving residents really needed.

For example, Texas Stadium, the world famous home of the Dallas Cowboys until 2008. Texas Stadium opened in 1971, a few years after the completed Irving comprehensive plan was abandoned unapproved by city officials, leaving future development throughout Irving completely open to interpretation, and not in a good way.

While the city's association with the Cowboys certainly produced significant tax revues in areas unavailable prior to building the stadium, one still must wonder if devoting the time, money and energy to this project was fair to Irving residents needing better city services and infrastructure; the residents who went without because local officials decided building and supporting the stadium was more important.

It seems obvious to me that the mindset at play on the city council in the late 60s-early 70s set the precedent for subsequent myopic, greedy decisions and poor judgment.

Greedy precedents my co-conspirators and I revolted against more than 20 years later - *an influential precedent we set* of which I am still proud; a resonance subsequent revolts utilized very effectively.

In 1996, after years of pressuring city council to improve and modernize Texas Stadium, including adding more opulent corporate skyboxes, completing the dome over the arena to provide climate control, improving and modernizing the fan experience with an adjoining amusement park, etc., the Cowboys owners participated in a significant effort to support a referendum in Irving to drop membership in Dallas Area Rapid Transit (DART).

Participation in DART requires paying a percentage of municipal tax revenues to fund mass transit service for Irving residents. In 1996, Cowboys owners wanted the money going to DART to instead fund improvements to Texas Stadium.

But, the people decided what *they* wanted.

Irving residents voted to stay in DART, choosing regional rapid transit instead of spending any more public money to accommodate the local millionaire-employing NFL franchise, eventually ending the city's professional relationship with the team.

The Cowboys still practice in Irving at their private facilities in Valley Ranch, but today all the big business of professional football is conducted to the west, down I-30, in the Cowboys' new $1.2 billion stadium in Arlington, a massive, lavish, gleaming structure made possible to a significant extent by public money.

Highest and best use? We'll see.

Joe B. Vaughan, Jr.

Conclusion

To be completely fair, there are two distinct types of developers in the world.

The first are hardworking, trying to make their livings bringing about projects that the rest of us need – places to live, places to purchase the things we want, places to drink coffee and write books about past political adventures. Stuff like that. These people are sensitive to their impact on the communities in which they work, and want to make life better for the rest of us with their plans and projects, if they can.

The second category is made up of scoundrels who believe they are owed massive profits, no matter who gets hurt in the process. They often scar the land with endless gulag-homage structures; cattle pens for the hypnotized zombies they perceive the rest of us to be. We sleepwalkers who deserve no better, our highest and best use being to pay rent and taxes to keep these vile developer bastards secure in massive, ornate houses, far from the sight of the gray dingy boxes they bring into the world and dump on the rest of us.

In my revolution, in this book, I was dealing with the latter category.

Not all revolutions have such strong images to motivate appropriate action. That by itself is probably a good thing. I would not wish the problems we rebelled against on anybody.

That fact doesn't negate the need to stand up and fight to get the government you deserve. Joining that fight means you no longer accept a town, a city, a state, a country where what seems logical and right to you and me seems unreasonable, undoable, unfathomable, too much trouble to the people we elect to represent us.

It means that whether our elected officials choose to accept it or not, our government must accommodate each of us. More. It means that while change takes time, we *expect* some goddamned results. And if we can't get them with the current batch of representatives, we'll find others. How hard could it be? Look at the ones we already have.

Ultimately, government, especially on the local level, must become a direct, faithful reflection of the governed. Any motivation in any politician other than that pure, responsive personation clouds that reflection, and after a point, nothing in the picture looks even remotely familiar. Distorted, alien, and incomprehensible.

Incapable of representation.

As my fellow revolutionary, I charge you then with this crucially important responsibility. Take control. Encourage everyone you know to do the same. It can be a massive pain in the ass, but much less so than allowing things to continue as they have - business as usual.

I found that out the hard way. After over 20 years of reckless overdevelopment, many of my co-conspirators wondered if our city could actually be saved; if the damage done wasn't already so severe, had gone on so long, that there was no cure.

If history proves that to be the case, then let this serve as an example of what happens when many good people simply stop paying attention to what is happening all around them.

Let it remind each of us that, as I mentioned previously, whether we participate or not our governments will continue operating, passing and enforcing laws, spending money possibly in unacceptable, disrespectful, contemptuous ways, and hoping that we never notice. That we never bother to find out. That we've decided it simply takes too much trouble to care.

Lead your revolution to keep this from happening. Or, if you revolt against a system already so nefarious and unresponsive that you must overthrow it completely and start again, remember that the more corrupt and broken a government is, the more apparent the need for remedy and the easier it will be to find many, many others like yourself ready and willing to make that important change.

That's what happened to me. I knew my government existed; it was out among the people needing the world to make some sense, to work in the correct way, far more powerful and inevitable than could ever be prevented by the lame puppets I found infesting my local government. My troops and I just had to show the rest of the good people around us there was a better way to run city hall.

That's the purpose of your movement, your revolution, your coup. To show all the people around you, your neighbors, your friends, that despite the tricks and subterfuge and thinly-veiled bullshit, logic, common sense, doing what needs to be done supersedes any political career, local or otherwise.

You are the boss and your politicians work for you. They exist to do your bidding, respond to your need, answer your call. *They represent you.* That's their job.

It's your right.

Joe B. Vaughan, Jr.